How many women are seeking pu ~~T000940~~ all there is to life?" *Reason to Return* answers: "You were made for so much more!" Ericka invites women to be who God made us to be by living an abundant life in a church community. Her words are refreshing and inspiring because they encourage us to "rewrite our faith stories." Ericka sees women as vital to church life because it is in our DNA to be life givers. And she encourages us to realize we have so much to receive inside "God's holy home on earth."

LINDA ZNACHKO, author and founder of He Knows Your Name

In the evangelical Western church, we inadvertently underestimate (and sometimes purposefully neglect) the communal aspect of our Christian faith. When we do, we miss out on meaningful community, embodied worship, and a historic and beautiful ecclesiology. If you've walked away from a church family or even the idea of church because of pain, trauma, shame, or flat-out annoyance, journalist Ericka Andersen is inviting you to reconsider coming home. While acknowledging the heartache that the Church has caused women, *Reason to Return* also reminds women of the deeper theological reasons why the Church desperately needs us—and why *we* still need the Church for our flourishing, growth, and purposes in God's Kingdom.

AUBREY SAMPSON, church planter and pastor at Renewal Church; speaker; and author of *Known*, *The Louder Song*, and *Overcomer*

In *Reason to Return*, Ericka Andersen honestly and delicately uncovers the spiritual woundings many of us have experienced in the local church while beautifully restoring the dignity of the Church at large. I especially appreciate Ericka's advocacy for the underserved in our church communities, most notably single mothers, who often feel unseen, unheard, and unwanted. For any woman desiring to encounter God more fully, reengagement in the local church is essential, and Ericka compassionately offers both renewed hope and practical guidance for safely navigating the experience.

MICHELLE DONNELLY, president and CEO of PlusONE Parents and author of *Save Haven*

Church is always and forever both highly personal and highly communal. In this book, Andersen boldly encourages us to keep asking Jesus for the right church balance in our lives. I found her arguments for being in church both convincing and encouraging.

TRACI RHOADES, author of *Not All Who Wander (Spiritually) Are Lost* and *Shaky Ground*

If you're like me, one of your deepest longings is to taste and see fresh evidence that we serve a living God—one who is actively making all things new. In *Reason to Return*, Ericka Andersen winsomely reminds us that the local church is the best place to find God at work, even if He's presently called us to a season of patient endurance. Engage with the local church, and you will find God on the move.

ANNA BROADWAY, author of *Sexless in the City*

In *Reason to Return*, Ericka casts a beautiful and compelling vision for women's commitment to a local body of believers. She reminds us of how vital being a part of an embodied community of Christians is, and she helps us navigate barriers to knowing and loving the bride of Christ.

CHELSEA SOBOLIK, ERLC director of public policy and author of *Longing for Motherhood*

Ministering to young, busy women in a post-Christian culture is challenging enough, but inviting the ones who have left back into a church community is downright daunting and intimidating. Ericka Andersen welcomes readers into her own spiritual journey—one of being raised in the Church, questioning the Church's methods, and then returning to the body of Christ. With truth and love, Andersen presents pragmatic, biblically based reasons why life lived in church fellowship is beneficial for individuals and the community. This book is a must-read for any woman questioning whether she can ever find her place in the Church again.

CHRISTINA CRENSHAW, PHD, associate researcher at the Hendricks Center at Dallas Theological Seminary and visiting fellow at Independent Women's Forum

Women are an integral and influential part of the body of Christ, necessary for the health of the Church. Ericka provides helpful insights into the alarming rate of women leaving the Church. She encourages women to consider what the Church still has to offer them—and what they can offer the Church. This is a necessary message for women today.

LAUREN MCAFEE, Ministry Investment Coordinator at Hobby Lobby Corporate and coauthor of *Only One Life* and *Not What You Think*

In our current culture, the Church is not known for its virtues. When stories of corruption and scandal seem to emerge every week, it's no wonder people are staying away. Thankfully, these stories of church failure are not the full picture. In pockets of faithfulness all over the world, God's people are showing up to be Jesus' hands and feet, and Ericka is telling this story. While the Church is not perfect, it is still a place of healing and calling, which is why I am so grateful to Ericka for beckoning women home.

SHARON HODDE MILLER, author of *The Cost of Control*

Why Women Need the Church
and the Church Needs Women

Reason *to* Return

ERICKA ANDERSEN

NavPress

A NavPress resource published in alliance
with Tyndale House Publishers

NavPress is the publishing ministry of The Navigators, an international Christian organization and leader in personal spiritual development. NavPress is committed to helping people grow spiritually and enjoy lives of meaning and hope through personal and group resources that are biblically rooted, culturally relevant, and highly practical.

For more information, visit NavPress.com.

Reason to Return: Why Women Need the Church and the Church Needs Women

Copyright © 2023 by Ericka Sylvester. All rights reserved.

A NavPress resource published in alliance with Tyndale House Publishers

NavPress and the NavPress logo are registered trademarks of NavPress, The Navigators, Colorado Springs, CO. *Tyndale* is a registered trademark of Tyndale House Ministries. Absence of ® in connection with marks of NavPress or other parties does not indicate an absence of registration of those marks.

The Team:
David Zimmerman, Publisher; Caitlyn Carlson, Acquisitions Editor; Deborah Sáenz Gonzalez, Developmental Editor; Elizabeth Schroll, Copy Editor; Olivia Eldredge, Operations Manager; Julie Chen, Designer; Sarah K. Johnson, Proofreader

Cover design and illustration by Julie Chen. Copyright © 2023 by Tyndale House Ministries. All rights reserved.

Author photo by Jenny Spires, copyright © 2022. All rights reserved.

Published in association with the literary agency of Legacy, LLC, 501 N. Orlando Avenue, Suite #313-348, Winter Park, FL 32789.

All Scripture quotations, unless otherwise indicated, are taken from the Holy Bible, *New International Version,*® *NIV.*® Copyright © 1973, 1978, 1984, 2011 by Biblica, Inc.® Used by permission. All rights reserved worldwide. Scripture quotations marked ESV are from The ESV® Bible (The Holy Bible, English Standard Version®), copyright © 2001 by Crossway, a publishing ministry of Good News Publishers. Used by permission. All rights reserved. Scripture quotations marked *NLT* are taken from the *Holy Bible*, New Living Translation, copyright © 1996, 2004, 2015 by Tyndale House Foundation. Used by permission of Tyndale House Publishers, Carol Stream, Illinois 60188. All rights reserved. Scripture quotations marked NKJV are taken from the New King James Version,® copyright © 1982 by Thomas Nelson. Used by permission. All rights reserved. Scripture quotations marked *MSG* are taken from *The Message,* copyright © 1993, 2002, 2018 by Eugene H. Peterson. Used by permission of NavPress. All rights reserved. Represented by Tyndale House Publishers. Scripture quotations marked KJV are taken from the *Holy Bible*, King James Version.

Some of the anecdotal illustrations in this book are true to life and are included with the permission of the persons involved. All other illustrations are composites of real situations, and any resemblance to people living or dead is purely coincidental.

For information about special discounts for bulk purchases, please contact Tyndale House Publishers at csresponse@tyndale.com, or call 1-855-277-9400.

ISBN 978-1-64158-566-8

Printed in the United States of America

29	28	27	26	25	24	23
7	6	5	4	3	2	1

This book is dedicated to the churches, pastors, ministry leaders, small groups, faithful friends, mission-trip buddies, and mentors who have helped me love God more through their presence, patience, and prayers.

Contents

PART THREE: A Call Worth Pursuing

Introduction

My first memories of church are perfumed by bleach and rosewood and patchouli. They are set in bright lights, intense overhead rectangles shining straight into corner cobwebs, illuminating dirt, decay, and the thinly skinned veins of dozens of octogenarians at a local nursing home. They sound like a neglected piano and the soprano voice of an eighty-year-old woman singing "His Eye Is on the Sparrow."[1] They feel like cold, crepey fingers reaching to touch mine as I look to my mom for reassurance to stay put. These memories echo as the seeds of Jesus and His Church—serving and communing among the vulnerable—planted in my mind. I didn't know then that I would forever be tugged back to these mornings, the ones that first shaped my understanding of what the Church is.

It began with my mom, who often packed up my sisters and me on Sundays—wrinkled dresses, tangled hair— depositing us in metal chairs next to people desperate for human touch while she went about setting up chairs, wheeling guests in from the hallway, and settling in our fellow congregants, born generations before her.

My mom is key to my understanding of church. She wasn't drawn to traditional services when I was young, but she has always been attracted to helping others. When she heard that the nursing home was looking for volunteers to participate in their Sunday services, she didn't hesitate. Not one for small talk, she wants a job to do in every situation, and this filled that desire.

After drifting from her faith as an adolescent, my mom searched to find her footing in faith again as a new mother. She knew the place to find it was in a church, but not necessarily the church of her youth. It had to be a church of her choosing, one where she could serve and be served.

Unconventional as it may sound, this nursing-home gathering was the church she needed at the time. She discovered a place that filled her need for fellowship, spirituality, and responsibility.

She found the opportunity to attend the nursing-home church through a bulletin board posting at another church. Something I will talk more extensively about later on in this book is how simply being in regular community at a church of some kind often leads to philanthropy, volunteerism, and generosity we might never encounter outside it. It's astounding how church attendance changes the trajectory of personal altruism.

I see now how my mom's intentional choice to seek out a personalized church model influenced me—influenced the subject matter of this book—so many years down the road. Through the lens of my mom's choice to participate in an unorthodox faith community, I began to see the true meaning of church. I recognized very early on that church didn't have to be one thing—that we could customize our faith lives to some extent. Mom didn't feel boxed in by someone else's expectation of what churchgoing should be. She did her own thing, as she always has, and it has profoundly influenced my own faith journey, with the local church at the center of it.

These days, nearly forty years later, my mom still doesn't miss a Sunday at church. She's *religious* about going, minus the rote, emotionless sense that often accompanies that word. It still fuels her action and fills her up, as it has since those early mornings in the nursing home. This solid consistency has contributed to a stronger faith for her—and fueled a life shaped by her own brand of humanitarianism. Generosity and volunteerism have defined my mom's life, and it's all sprouted from a deep love for people, a love that God planted in her through His Church.

While my mom's example in my childhood left a lasting impression on me, someone else made an even bigger imprint on how I would eventually view the Church and those proximate to it. Prior to a few years ago, I never realized that the local church was such a vital component of a rich faith life. If you look at the life of Jesus, however, you can see that it is. He was always with a group of people—whether close friends, disciples, or curious bystanders.

He sat with strangers, dined with thieves, conversed with murderers. Those same ragtag groups of people exist today. They are me, they are you, they are our fellow churchgoers, friends, and neighbors. We aren't too good to dine with them, love them, or (if need be) forgive them. And I hope they think the same of us.

If imperfect communion with sinners and saints was something Jesus pursued, it's most certainly something we should echo. It's also where we *are needed*. As members of the body of Christ, we each have an indispensable role to play—just as my mom did serving those in the nursing home.

If you've been absent from the Church—either physically or spiritually—an important piece of your faith life is missing. Do you want to discover where you fit in, again or for the first time? Do you want to bypass the obligations of religion and dive into a deeper, more satisfying life in Jesus? That's why I wrote this book. When I drifted, I needed an anchor. When I desired a closer relationship with God, I needed guidance. When I stepped away from my church, I needed a reason to come back. That's why I wrote this—for you.

PART ONE

The Reasons We Leave

CHAPTER 1

Our Desires

SEARCHING FOR MORE

It was 10:00 p.m., and my three-year-old wouldn't go to sleep. She'd already been read seven books, had two sips of water, and switched pajamas twice. Her unicorn stuffie and doll were tucked in beside her. Her rainbow-sparkled comforter was molded tightly around her tiny body just as she liked, but her brain was spinning from the bowl of ice cream she'd had two hours earlier. No matter how many steps we took to prepare for it, she refused to move toward sleep.

As a tired mom wanting desperately to escape to my room for a few minutes of reading, I began pleading with her. These sleeping issues have been going on most of her life. I know that when she pushes against sleep, it's bad for her. She doesn't understand this now, but as an adult who has researched health data about children, I know that they need a certain number of hours each night in order to function well during the day. When kids are rested, they are happier, learn more easily, and have fewer meltdowns.

I know I can't expect my toddler to understand this, but even still, it's maddening when she fights against it!

One day it became obvious to me that as Christians we act toward our faith like my toddler does toward sleep. We comprehend why we should take certain actions for our own well-being and spiritual growth, but oftentimes it's hard to actually put these actions into practice.

Going to church, being part of a faith community, is one of the actions that many adult Christians struggle to accomplish. Many have given up entirely, despite knowing that having a strong faith life is more difficult and lacking without it. Women in particular have left the Church at high rates, despite still considering themselves to be dedicated Christians. At one point in my life, I was one of them.

Having grown up in Christian culture, I'm well versed in the religious platitudes that come with this kind of upbringing. For a long time, that's all Christianity was to me. But I reached a certain age where I knew there must be a deeper, more significant faith life to be found beyond rules of dos and don'ts. What was the secret? How could I find the deeper spiritual fulfillment that eluded me—even though I'd attended church most of my life?

For a while, that meant stepping away from church and

reevaluating the point of it all. Why was I going? What was it for? Was it really helping me grow as a Christian? Was it worth the time and commitment I'd once put into it? This book was part of my process of evaluating these questions and finding answers I hadn't been sure were available.

If you don't currently attend a church, you're likely still one of millions of American women aspiring to deeper spiritual fulfillment.

As a journalist covering issues of faith and culture, I recently discovered some information about church and our faith practices that I hadn't known before. I was shocked to learn that twenty-six million American women who attended church a decade ago no longer do.[1]

What happened? Why have so many women stopped going to church? Research indicates that many of them still consider themselves to be Christians, but a myriad of life circumstances has launched a trend of declining attendance, only now compounded by the COVID-19 pandemic. The first part of this book explores many of these circumstances— the reasons women have left.

As I researched this phenomenon, I also uncovered that there are massive benefits to being an active member of a church. They are personal, practical, and spiritual in nature—and you may be surprised at how they are manifested, especially for women.

Research shows that people of faith—especially those who attend church consistently—have the lowest rates of depression and highest rates of happiness in the nation.[2] So when

Christian women aren't attending church, they're missing out on a tangible benefit that church community provides. It's crazy to think that this can make the difference that it does, but it's true.

Can going to church really change your life? Maybe you've gone plenty of times before and are looking for something more this time, something worth it. It can be overwhelming—this intangible desire for something greater that's hard to explain or grasp. Understandably, you may not be sure how or where to even begin, especially if your past pursuits have failed.

You may have tried it all: different types of churches or denominations, self-help books, prayer journals, meditation practices. You may have seen it all: hypocrisy, legalism, lies. You may have felt it all: doubt, disappointment, hopelessness.

Others seem to enjoy flourishing, confident faith lives, but it's hard to discern what provides their fulfillment. You're not alone in wondering what's missing or desiring a deeper faith life, one that reflects a personal relationship with God.

For you, is it the Church itself that has lost its luster or is it a "dead orthodoxy" or "worldly Christianity" that no longer appeals to you?[3] Taking the time to really nail down what's turned you off in the past is important in this journey.

In their book *Churchless*, David Kinnaman and George Barna report that half of people not currently attending church in the US are "actively seeking something better spiritually than they have experienced to date."[4] One-third of those say that they are "completely open" to trying a new or atypical church structure or environment.[5] Why *not* try something new? It's the direction many people are headed and something to consider for yourself.

Consideration and action, however, are two very different things. Apprehension about trying a new church environment and taking regular action to deepen your faith could be hindering the very growth you seek. So let's talk about the elephant in the room: What is church? What does the word mean, and why can it be such a sensitive subject?

Let's start with God's Word. The Bible is packed with tales of Jesus seeking out followers in both traditional and nontraditional faith environments. Sometimes He consorted with them in the Temple. Other times He just walked up to where they already happened to be—working a boat or mending some nets. Many of the disciples were fishing, oblivious that their lives were about to be upended, when He approached them. Mary's everyday life was interrupted by the angel Gabriel. Zacchaeus was in a tree with no idea what was to come. Such encounters—in spaces and places as conventional as a temple and untraditional as a tree—are the nature of the Church still today.

What Is Church?

The word *church* may elicit many visions: A symmetrical white structure crowned by a large cross. Light-up signage displaying service times and a bad pun ("Our Sundays are better than Dairy Queen's"). Or maybe a tiny church house surrounded by farm country with a gravel parking lot bordering a three-step jaunt to double doors. Perhaps a megachurch island, stretching for three corners of a block and requiring police presence to guide the legions of traffic going in and out of the football stadium–sized parking lot encasing it like a moat.

For traditionalists, it's suits and hats. For millennials, it's a coffee bar and donuts. For fundamentalists, it's fire and brimstone. For Gen Z, it's livestreams and pajamas. But church is so much more than all that.

Because I want to make sure we're on the same page throughout our time together, let me set the parameters for what I mean by *church*. The big-C Church is the global body of believers, including millions of men and women scattered around the world. This larger, symbolic body gathers in God's name and serves as our eternal shelter in a broken world. It's anywhere and everywhere believers reside, wherever "two or three gather in [Jesus'] name" (Matthew 18:20). I'll refer to this as "the Church."

The second meaning I'll refer to, more frequently, is that of the little-c church. This is what I'll call the local church throughout the book. Here I'll be talking about one of many particular church congregations of Christians who traditionally gather each week. The little-c church is part of the big-C Church and functions simultaneously as both. As Christians, we can participate in both entities.

Both the Church and the local church are holy gatherings of two or more people specifically meaning to glorify God—to hear from Him, worship Him, and align their hearts with His.

Historically speaking, one common use of the term *church* is a translation mishap. This word was never meant to refer to a building or place but rather a gathering of people. It's a translation of the word *ekklēsia*, which describes this specific kind of gathering.[6]

I love how Sam Allberry explains the church operating in the earthly world:

> The church functions like an embassy of this new society that God is creating through Christ. Just as the US embassy in London is considered a part of US sovereign territory overseas in a foreign land, so the local church is a small part of heavenly territory in this world.[7]

It is holy ground. The Church and the local church are not about a day of the week or a building to walk into but about a people and a way of life. "People don't enter a church; the church enters a building," writes Allberry.[8]

This reality often gets fuzzy because of our tangible understanding of the Church as a specific gathering *place*. It is this, in a sense, because we sometimes just need a practical place to meet, but it's critical that we comprehend the Church as God originally intended if we are to know why it's so essential in our lives as Christians.

I recently saw a great visualization of this. It was a drawing of a cross section of a downtown area with a few stores, a couple of high-rise apartment buildings, a park bench, sidewalks, families, and shoppers. At the top, it read, "Where the Church Is" and had arrows pointing at each person, object, and building. We may have buildings to gather in, but the heart of the Christian Church resides exclusively in the fellowship of believers, wherever they are at any time.

Local church members' work among one another and in their communities is often done outside the walls of church buildings throughout the week as they come together as servants, friends, and community members. We must always have the larger perspective of the Church in mind whenever talking about individual churches.

When I was a kid, church was a building to me, as it may have been to you. It was tights, hymnals, and flannel boards. It wasn't until years later that I learned the point of it all, the actual definition and origins of this place, as we've just covered.

Now that we're straight on that, let's talk about what church could look like for you moving forward.

If you are feeling led to something new or called to revisit a cornerstone of your past in a new light, that's a great place to be. It's possible you've grown out of what you used to know. Your past contours no longer fit here—and that's okay. In *The Problem of Pain*, C. S. Lewis writes,

> If all experienced God in the same way and returned Him an identical worship, the song of the Church triumphant would have no symphony, it would be like an orchestra in which all the instruments played the same note.[9]

Sometimes the symphony needs a fresh sound. And that might be what you have to offer.

Maybe you'll relate to this: Twenty years ago, I was a young adult with every dream and desire before me. Feeling invincible, I did things during that time I can't imagine doing now: I flew to India on a whim, went skydiving after a night of heavy drinking, and moved to a city I'd never been to without a job in place—just for the fun of it. Now, as a married, midcareer mom of two, my church and spiritual needs are quite different from what they once were.

We can shift into new gears in our personal lives *and* our faith lives. In fact, these two aspects of our lives can and should ultimately merge together. As Christians, we want to hold our jobs and hobbies and circumstances loosely, but it's possible to reconfigure the pieces to uphold what we value most in a healthy way. Can you allow yourself the space to shift in different life seasons? We're meant to find fresh resources and rituals as time passes. We can't blossom in old, untilled soil—so let's stop trying to! It's time for some soil rejuvenation or a new pot altogether.

So much can change over the course of our lives, but one thing never does: God's love and His call to fellowship. We'll explore this unchanging truth further; it's essential in developing fruitful habits that lead to the spiritual fulfillment you seek.

There may be baggage in your life. There may be fear, doubt, confusion, or ambivalence. Perhaps there is regret, harm, or sheer disinterest. You may not hold a lot of hope that going to church can make a drastic difference. We're going to address all these things, friend. As someone who has walked through this myself and stood beside others on the journey, I'm honored to accompany you as you tread lightly into this territory again.

Facing the Church: Reconsidering How It Fits

When it comes to your faith, what have you been putting into practice? An online sermon on occasion? Attending your old church on holidays? Keeping up with your favorite Christian podcast? Praying—sometimes? Are these things taking you to the place you'd like to be? These can no doubt be helpful and edifying tools to aid your spiritual life, but I wonder if they're enough for you. If not, can you make the time to figure out what might be? (If you're reading this book, you're doing just that.)

The hesitation is real, though—I get it. You dread the inevitable burst of new conversation that comes with entering a new church or trying a new space week after week. You may worry that church members will judge strangers and may not be prepared to deal with emotionally stressful situations. Maybe you consider the churches of your past and wonder if another could ever be different. You may have believed so deeply in God and His goodness that being treated badly in a church made it feel like God was absent from that place. If that was the case, leaving was probably the right choice!

This legitimate discomfort or hurt you fear encountering again is Satan's attempt to thwart God's plan for you. I don't want Satan's tactics to keep you from experiencing the wonder, mercy, and solace of what God means for the Church to be in your life.

God says in Jeremiah 7:11 (NLT): "Don't you yourselves admit that this Temple, which bears my name, has become a den of thieves?" Even in the holiest places, sometimes sin corrupts. *And yet.* As He always does, despite the tarnishing of His own name and the betrayal of His people, God still calls the Church His beloved. He is not bound by the walls of a building, the reputation of any pastor, or the sins we commit.

Why let a tarnished definition of the Church limit our vision of what it is and can be? What if the Church isn't what you've been thinking it is all these years? What if your history with the Church is merely one example among many . . . and it doesn't represent the truth of who God is? By reading this book, you've demonstrated a level of commitment to figuring this out for yourself. What priorities may need to shift for you to experience the Church as the *more* you've been looking for?

CHAPTER 2

Our Time

Life started to get crazy when my son entered kindergarten. This was very unlike the early parts of his life, when I'd often been bored with endless hours to fill, blessed and burdened with the toils of new motherhood. Fast-forward a few years—throw a little sister and preschool into the mix—and things got wild.

With the start of kindergarten came a stricter schedule, extracurricular activities, and a daily struggle to get dinner on the table and get the kids to bed by 8:00 p.m. for a 6:00 a.m. wake-up call the next day. Time wasn't our friend, and the stress of the working-parent life encroached on us as it hadn't before.

Most people—parents or not—can relate to feeling

overwhelmed by commitments. It's one of the main reasons many families stop attending church regularly—if they ever began going at all. As soccer and baseball games intrude, schedules and minutes are dictated by school and practice. Or the week is so packed that it's just nice to relax without obligations on Sundays.

It's easy to let faith habits slide into the background. This shifting of priorities might not make a noticeable difference in your life immediately, but successive weeks, months, and years of abandoned faith practices begin to carve out an emptiness, a wanting. Have you felt it? Even if you haven't fully left the Church, maybe something in that area of your heart is amiss. I know it was for me, yet I struggled to know exactly what this "something" was.

Maybe you, as I was (and often still am!), are part of the majority of American women who identify as stressed and tired.[1] How about overcommitted or dissatisfied? Mothers specifically—followed by women generally—report the highest numbers in these areas. Most women say they want to do better in at least one life area.[2] Some set work, parenting, marital, or friendship goals as their top priority, but the primary way most women would like to see positive change in their lives is in church activity and personal faith.[3]

With every last drop of ourselves squeezed into family life and work obligations, it can feel impossible to even begin thinking about meaningful change on such a deep level. Our faith usually gets whatever energy is left over when the kids are in bed, the dogs are quieted, and the computer is shut down.

But very little moves forward on the power of fading fumes. When prioritizing our faith is something we put off for "when things calm down" or when we're in the right headspace to think clearly, it doesn't happen at all. It becomes cached and categorized in some dusty mental file that you hope to open . . . someday.

Been there, girl! I'm a working mom of two who's more likely to say yes than no to requests and prone to taking on mentorships and meal making when I really . . . just . . . can't. I'm not just trying to stay above water as a mom but also invest in my marriage, volunteer in the community, keep my bosses happy, check in with friends, and try to make space every day for a rich and growing spiritual life.

The hamster wheel isn't joyless, but it's jam-packed and very difficult to turn off for even a moment. I know "Keep the Sabbath Day holy" is the commandment I'm most likely to break—even when I do go to church. Yet I know that going to church is one of the foundational and most significant things I can do to ground my faith.

Going to church doesn't define our faith, but the weekly ritual *can* reignite our commitment to a God-centered life. It can also help build a solid faith life for your family moving forward.

It's been so important for me that I can't help but want to tell you more about why. I don't want you to miss out. If you are a sister in Christ, a mom, or a woman who doesn't fit either of these categories, this is for you.

Why Making Time Matters

For most of my life, I never thought twice about what it meant to attend church regularly—it's just what we did as a family. Now I can see how this weekly custom grounded my spirituality and helped build the faith I have today.

Sometimes it can seem like the Christian faith is boxed in. It is often defined by uttering one prayer of salvation. But there is much more to it than that. If, as Christians, we really want to experience meaning here on earth, a holistic approach with the local church as the centerfold is the way. Why? Because our relationship with God shouldn't just be a slice of our lives—compartmentalized into a box—but an integrated part of our physical, emotional, social, and spiritual well-being. When it's not, things can feel "off." That makes sense if *the* Source of our life is relegated to the same status as several other sources we pull from.

As one writer put it, "A Holistic Faith Lifestyle realizes God is deeply connected to every part of our mind, body, and spirit as well as the world in which we live."[4] The truth is, we were made for worship and communion with God, so when that's not the basis of how we live, we're naturally out of alignment on a soul level.

There are varying definitions of *holistic*, but simply put: When our faith is holistic, Christianity is interconnected to everything we do. God has given us some clear ways to ensure we embody and express our faith as He intends. One of the most foundational ways is by meeting and encouraging one another, as we're instructed to do in Hebrews 10:24-25:

Let us consider how we may spur one another on . . .
not giving up meeting together, as some are in the
habit of doing, but encouraging one another—and
all the more as you see the Day approaching.

When we live in such a way, with core components of a holistic faith at the forefront, the result is a supernatural satisfaction and fulfillment. That doesn't mean it's easy. But when
something truly matters, the effort put forth is invaluable. It's
worth the effort to pursue a deeper relationship with God in
this way. It's worth it so we experience abundant life on earth
and create pathways for an even greater eternity in heaven.
What will it take to make the time in your life?

Skip the Hacks

In the brain scramble of a busy life, it's perfectly understand-
able to temporarily forget how or what you've built your
faith on. We want the ease of a quick fix, to cross something
off our to-do list and move on to the next thing. That is so
me. But there are no twenty-minute TED Talks with all the
answers, no spiritual supplements to ingest and speed up the
process. Google can help, but heart issues simply don't have
purchasable solutions.

I've certainly tried to solve my own problems this way,
taking online courses on everything from public speaking
to entrepreneurship. I've also taken SuperGreen supplements out of a desire not to eat vegetables. We want all the
shortcuts—to take every action but the hardest ones, the

ones that will actually move the needle: time, intention, and real-life experience.

Trying to skip the line never works. It's like reading the CliffsNotes instead of a classic novel—you'll walk away with only a shallow understanding of the full masterpiece. "Using a shortcut . . . does not honor the learning process," writes Jen Wilkin in *Women of the Word*, where she urges women to go directly to the Bible instead of always relying on devotional interpretations of Scripture.[5] Sometimes it's easier to read a glitzy devotional than the meaty verses of Deuteronomy. But it's not nearly as beneficial. The same is true of other faith habits. We all want to take the easy way sometimes, but we're selling ourselves short by not pursuing the real thing.

As it is with our bodies and minds (pills and podcasts only take us so far), so it is with our hearts and souls. Slow, intentional choices are the way. In accepting this, we can begin to move forward.

As I near my forties, I'm finally *getting* that breath; sunlight, crisp air, and lavender bathwater really are nourishing and life-giving. It took removing my ego, halting my personal rat race, and filtering out the junk to receive that blessing.

Pressing stop on all the things can seem impossible. And I know that finding a pathway back to a place where faith is a central tenet of your life can feel loaded and difficult. But it doesn't have to be. It comes down to keeping relationships—with God and with brothers and sisters in Christ—at the heart of your pursuit.

Putting in the time and effort that meaningful relationships with God and other believers require will change your life. Even better? These are the most important relationships you'll ever have. They will ground and guide the entirety of your life. Not just yours, but those of your family members and communities as well. The light of God in someone (in this case, you!) is too bright not to spill over into every other part of their life. When we are in Christ, we are the light of the world. So get ready to shine, baby.

Many women have let their faith and connections to the local church drift. But Christians who cling to the truth of gospel hope and biblical community preserve our faith for future generations. Making time to build a stronger faith is not just important but essential to fulfillling our larger purpose. Fostering relationships with God and those in the Church in practical ways is the start.

Become Friends with God

Start at square one—your basic, foundational relationship with God. It can be easy to view this relationship as something more ethereal than necessary. A long time ago, I started praying a lot more honestly and authentically, chatting it up with God like a friend on my work commutes or over my morning coffee. I do respect Him as holy, to be revered, but He is omnipotent in His ability to be friend and Father simultaneously.

Consider how you view other relationships in your life to see how the one you have with God compares with those. You can maintain a long-distance relationship or friendship over the course of years. For example, I have a few friends from college I rarely speak to whom I still consider good friends even though I see them rarely. But could I tell you how their lives are really going? Am I the one they call when their kid is diagnosed with a learning disability and their husband checks out? Do they call me to see how my kids' first week at day care went? Nope. It feels good to reconnect on special occasions, but our relationship is surface level because we aren't in community with one another. They don't carry me when things are hardest—or know when I'm celebrating small victories. They are great fixtures, we have good memories, and I wouldn't give them up for the world, but we'd be closer if we lived nearby, spoke daily, and got together regularly.

On the other hand, there's my best friend. When she's struggling as a mom, it's a 911 call that I make time to pick up. When she feels inadequate or fearful about a new project, I'm on it. When work frustrations leave me unsure of what to do next, she talks me through them. She even has the authority to call me out on bad behavior because I trust her love for me and desire for my well-being. I'm grateful to have such a friend in my life; they aren't easy to come by.

Our relationship is strong because we put work into it. We don't always agree. We've had our rough patches. I've said some nearly unforgivable things at times. But because our relationship is based in mutual love, respect, and an overarching understanding of long-term investment, we've gotten through those things. Our friendship stands solid on the truth of what we know about one another and is rooted in love. We have shared memories of our time as roommates and young professionals and of our quests for love and marriage, and she was the first person I called the moment I went into labor with my first child. We know each other's spouses and children. Because of all these things, our friendship is a close one with deep meaning.

Now imagine if we only ever spoke on the phone for five minutes at a time without experiencing anything in person together—or if we weren't familiar with each other's family members and other loved ones. Our relationship would be shallow.

Pastor Dr. Tony Evans put it this way on Twitter:

> I hear people say, "I don't have to go to church to be a Christian," and they are absolutely right. Salvation is through faith alone in Christ alone. But you don't have to go home to be married, but stay away long enough & your relationship will be affected.[6]

It's also like that when we don't get to know God's family. It doesn't feel like you know Him well (and you certainly won't) when you don't take the time to get to know His family, those in the Church. In Ephesians 2:19 (ESV), we read: "You are no longer strangers and aliens, but you are fellow citizens with the saints and members of the household of God."

If we are friends with God, we are no longer strangers to other members of His household. We are fellow citizens—and what do fellow citizens do? They gather, speak, love, and build a better city together. They make time for what matters to them as a community, and, in turn, serve and love their leaders and community more effectively. Focusing on this higher priority will help us filter out the less important parts of life.

And unlike with the superfoods and master classes I mentioned earlier, there is no charge for a more valuable relationship with God and a loving faith community. It's free—yet priceless. It's available to everyone, even those battling complicated faith histories and unavoidable responsibilities that make things more difficult.

Since you are reading this book, something inside you may be urging you to get back to church and begin restoring your faith. You'd like a better relationship with God, a stronger spiritual life, a growing faith foundation for your kids. Maybe you've tried to shake it off, but it keeps coming back. The yearning beats with your heart and whispers in your ear. At some point, it might be time to admit that God's trying to send you a message.

If you are resistant to this due to previous negative experiences, I have good news: Those things can help you steer clear of toxic environments as you choose something new.

It can be difficult to talk yourself into attending an unfamiliar church, but it may be exactly what you need to find the God you've been missing. Don't get me wrong: God is here with you too—in your living room or car, your laundry room or backyard. He'll meet you in the middle of the ocean or at the top of a mountain. He'll go anywhere to find

His lost sheep, leaving the rest of them behind to save the one (Matthew 18:12). But God's presence is felt in a transcendent way when His people gather.

We know this because He has told us so. When Jesus was here on earth, He did much "to equip the saints for the work of ministry, for building up the body of Christ" (see Ephesians 4:12, ESV). The body of Christ is the Church! That means the big-C Church—as in, the global body of believers. It's also the little-c (local) church, the people located in our specific geographic communities who often meet inside a church building on Sundays. The body of Christ is you and me, friend—and we've got an important calling to participate in.

I know it can be overwhelming to find a new church or start attending again. But stick with me as we journey through the reasons it's worth it. If the past several years have taught me anything, it's that.

CHAPTER 3

Our Misconceptions

"I don't go to church," my new friend said. "I have my own relationship with God. Church is just toxic." It was something I'd heard before, this common refrain of a personal connection to God being sufficient. At one point, I'd merely considered it personal preference. But the more I've learned about the nature of healing, the holistic components of a deep faith, and the power of a spiritual community, the more I've seen some of the downfalls of siloed communion with God. They aren't obvious at first, though, and I didn't think much about this until a few years ago. But now I know what an incredible blessing it is to thoroughly breathe in the fullness of God's nature, which is experienced best in the presence of others. It's too much for one person to hold—as are the many pains and problems that crowd our lives.

Maybe you've thought that you don't need church to have a relationship with God. Or you've heard others say something similar. Most Sundays, my dad believed it—a sentiment that rose from the rumble of his motorcycle engine warming up for a midmorning cruise.

But where did that mindset come from? Strangely, churchgoing Christians themselves gave rise to it. In the mid-twentieth century, evangelical Christianity moved away from emphasizing public professions of faith experienced in community to focusing on believers' personal relationships with Jesus. The shift is often tied to legendary preacher Billy Graham and his crusades, which highlighted this personal relationship. I have much respect for Graham and what he did, and I'm not sure this ultimate result was his intention. But into the twenty-first century, evangelical Christianity has focused less and less on communal acts.

To be clear, yes, a personal relationship with Jesus is essential to our faith. But if that alone were all that God called us to as Christians, most of the Bible would be unnecessary. So much of it is about living *with* people and loving them well through forgiveness and compassion and justice.

And here's the truth: You can certainly connect with God while flying down an interstate on a sunny day or hear Him between your reps at the gym, working out life in the grunts and glory of these earthly things. God is omnipotent and omnipresent, painted into the still life on your walls, rising in the steam from your French press coffee, animated in the smile of your toddler. There's no doubt: You *can* have a relationship with Him beyond the confines of a church building. We should recognize Him—*acknowledge* Him—in the great and small wonders of the world. Also? While it can sometimes feel like a church is a barrier, it's actually the gateway. There's so much missing when you worship solo.

Once any of us begins a personal relationship with Jesus, we are bestowed with the sacred responsibility to love our neighbors and walk through trials and tribulations with others in our faith community. It's a mercy that we are saved by grace, but God has never suggested that we should stop there.

The Old Testament is full of His lamentations at His people for casting aside justice for the weak and vulnerable. It sometimes seems like people want to ignore the Old Testament as if nothing it says matters anymore. Yes, Jesus saved us—thank God—but the Old Testament God *is* the New Testament God. His call for selflessness, obedience, and care for the vulnerable is clear.

The Bible is *all about* community. The Israelites are rarely singled out as individuals, and there are constant references to God's people, not "God's person." We are individual creations with unique qualities, but we've got zero indication that God wants us to live out our faith alone. As it says in Isaiah 1:17,

Learn to do right; seek justice.
    Defend the oppressed.
Take up the cause of the fatherless;
    plead the case of the widow.

His Spirit moves through the faithful to accomplish justice on earth, and if we aren't making ourselves available to that by being in community, we are disobeying His will.

It's in groups of people where we see some of God's greatest miracles—the parting of the Red Sea, the feeding of the five thousand, Jesus' death and resurrection. These things are *never* solitary. And yet when we exclude ourselves from the community of God, we can easily miss the miracles and opportunities to be part of a story greater than ourselves. Don't miss your part in the Greatest Story Ever Told.

I get it: It's not a church you want but more of God. That's the rub—more of church *is* more of God. The Church, in all its iterations, is His home. As you've probably felt, seeking God independently is dissatisfying. And if the one thing women want to prioritize more in their life is faith and church, we need to understand how that's done.[1]

Yes, a personal relationship with God is the foundation. But how do we grow beyond infancy in our faith? We can listen to a podcast or catch a sermon online, but it's not sufficient. "The difference between listening to a radio sermon and going to church," said theologian D. L. Moody, "is almost like the difference between calling your girl on the phone and spending an evening with her."

We can start where we are and get honest with God about our desire, asking Him to guide us toward the right people, the right local church. He is trustworthy to guide us in all our endeavors.

The good news about the Good News—that Jesus died to save us from our sins—is that it *never* changes. A bonus part of the Good News is that we get a built-in international family the moment we place our faith in Christ. Get to know your family, and you'll become more confident in God's promises for your life. These people will speak into you, revealing new dimensions of the Father—things unseen without the additional light that fellow believers bring with them.

Today you are exactly where you are supposed to be, and God is sovereign. He could have brought you here before, but He didn't. Is now the time? Are you ready for spiritual renewal? I believe that picking up this book was a sign that the answer is yes. I believe God brought us together on this very page. I am overwhelmed with love for the life you've been called to live in Him. Are you ready to learn more about how to make it so?

Finding Renewal

When I consider renewal, a few things come to mind: a fresh blanket of snow, a perfectly unwrinkled bedspread, a pink-skinned newborn howling at the dazzling world for the very first time. Today that newborn is you, brought to a place where the stories you've been telling yourself about life and heart and spirit are under analysis.

We humans are layered, nuanced, spiritual, complicated, beautiful souls, and the components of life don't come with instructions. But I'm so glad you're here, courageously taking a step toward the One you know is good. You are in a *great* space. Being curious and anticipatory, halfway believing that God is going to show up? That's it.

And, by the way, He is going to show up. It's time to process the Church as it exists in your mind, as it's embedded into your body from years past, as it will fill you in the future. Let's review the good, bad, and ugly, and then filter out what's no longer helpful for you.

Listening Closely

The best way to get a good seat at the table is to listen. Rarely do we find transformation in relationship and spirit by looking inward. Transformation happens when we look upward and outward, going beyond our own little lives to recognize something deeper than ourselves. There's always a bigger story. God is sovereign, but He's got specific jobs for each of us as part of His Kingdom. And He's always had special ways of speaking to His people.

I'm not saying that someone can't hear from God while running errands on a Tuesday with a podcast turned up in their earbuds. But without our conscious choice to open ourselves up to His voice, it will be harder to hear.

In isolation, apart from our brothers and sisters in Christ, it's easier to ignore heavenly callings to love and service. It may be easier to go it alone, to write a check and be done with it, choosing not to deal with the messiness of our fellow Christians, but that isn't worth it in the end. If money was all that was needed, the world wouldn't be in such a tragic state.

CHAPTER 4

Our Understanding

WHAT IS THE CHURCH TO US?

Depending on your family history, your cultural background, and where you grew up, the word *church* can produce vastly different visions. In the South, most people grew up attending church weekly, or at least frequently. Midwesterners are also known to be regular churchgoers. Maybe you were invited to Vacation Bible Schools in the summer or youth-group trips in the fall. Maybe you joined a group with Campus Life (a popular high school Christian ministry) or commonly saw kids praying around a flagpole a few times a year.[1]

Perhaps you grew up Catholic, getting baptized as an infant and taking Holy Communion at seven, and a tiny photo of you in a white gown is still stashed in a box somewhere at your parents' house. If you hail from the Northwest or Northeast, church might be less familiar to you. Some have labeled these locations post-Christian, and it's common for kids to grow up in them not having talked about or ever gone to church.

Regardless of your childhood experience, church is rarely a neutral topic and is often (understandably) charged with emotional recollections or opinions.

Many are familiar with the effervescent smile of Joel Osteen flashing across a TV screen. Churches like Osteen's are the largest, most easily identified cultural markers of church today, but 70 percent of US churches have one hundred or fewer regular attendees.[2] Many people are part of one of tens of thousands of smaller congregations scattered across the country. Maybe your childhood church is one of them. And maybe you have an experience a bit like my own.

My Church Story

I've been going to church since I was three years old. A standard wardrobe rises to memory: ruby-red-heart-stitched thick white tights and shiny plastic shoes with miniature buckles and plenty of scuff marks. Back then, we went to a charismatic Pentecostal church. Each week for church pick-ups, my grandma drove an elongated church bus scribbled with "Assemblies of God" on the door. She usually dropped by our pothole-riddled, six-house neighborhood, where my sisters and I piled in for a wild ride. This was the 1980s, before there were stringent car seat rules for children older than toddlers. So we got comfy in the vinyl seats and were soon joined by college students and an assortment of other colorful churchgoers.

We usually wore our best (which for me often meant a clearance dress from Kmart) and looked forward to stale animal crackers and tiny cups of juice at snack time. Incorporated were the classic symbols of yesteryear's Sunday school: the Noah's Ark flannel board, passionate versions of "I've Got the Joy, Joy, Joy, Joy (Down in My Heart)," and annual Christmas pageants—where I always hoped to play Mary but ended up a shepherd, an innkeeper, or worse, just part of the choir.

I "accepted Jesus into my heart" around the age of seven or eight. The details we often remember from the many millions of moments of our lives are so select. What is stored in my mind from that day is this: the memory of sitting with my back against the wall near the classroom door in that now-long-lost Easter dress of my youth. During class, we had shared prayer requests, and I had offered one that I just knew God would answer. My grandma, the one who had driven us to church that very morning, had cancer. She had lost her hair. She had a fluffy wig that was supposed to look like her real hair but obviously wasn't. Her baggy T-shirts hung more loosely than before, and her cheek bones jutted upward like socket wrenches. She was only fifty years old, and we needed her for a whole lot longer than this. Perhaps my belief that God could cure Grandma's cancer led me to step into a real relationship with Him one Sunday morning.

I was compelled to believe in Jesus, this friendly man who "loved the little children" and made the blind see, the lame walk, the sick well, the outcast loved, and the murderer miraculously forgiven. If not Jesus, then who? Faith felt big, even as a seven-year-old.

It's easy to write off an early childhood conversion—and people do. I certainly had a lot to learn and would go through many tests of faith, but I still believe that that was the day I began to love Christ as I do today. It felt personal. It felt authentic. It felt eternal, in as deep a way as a little girl can experience. Those feelings were eventually confirmed by evidence as I grew to understand the truth behind Christianity's claims and the reasons we can put our trust in Jesus. But at that moment, as I'm sure my grandma herself had already prayed for, the Holy Spirit moved me to belief in Him.

My relationship with Jesus began inside the classroom of a church building. The foundation on which my entire life is built began that day . . . because I was at church.

Changing Faith

It's not uncommon to hear about people who experienced a certain kind of church growing up and then reached a point in their adolescence or adulthood when that type of church was no longer meaningful to them. Sometimes it's our belief in God that is in question, and other times it's simply our experience of a specific type of church. Because of the changing nature of life and faith, it's important to think about our understanding of church as it relates to the reasons we have left.

The global pandemic has had a significant impact on many

Christians' relationship to and understanding of the Church. Many people stopped attending for what they thought would be a few weeks but turned out to be a few years. Some churches began streaming services online. Large churches have been hit the hardest. These gleaming white structures, often spanning an entire block of a local suburb, sat rattling with dusty Sunday school toys, unused paper coffee cups, and yet-to-be-cracked-open Bibles for more than a year. No matter how great your online streaming service may be, it cannot replace the power of flesh-and-blood community. Yet nearly two years into the pandemic, one large church near my house still had not reopened for in-person services. This worldwide calamity has caused people to reevaluate what they want in a church—and if they want to go to church at all.

The silver lining of the pandemic is that it has urged people to begin thinking more deeply and making more intentional choices about the deeper parts of their lives. It has initiated a pruning of God's people and shaped more fruitful local churches that offer renewed vibrancy in the lives of their members. Researcher Ed Stetzer's response to a 2015 Pew Research survey describes our current reality:

> Christianity isn't collapsing; it's being clarified.
> Churches aren't emptying; rather, those who were
> Christian in name only are now categorically
> identifying their lack of Christian conviction and
> engagement.[3]

A revitalized Church is being built as we speak! God is going to do so much with it, and you are invited to participate. What will this mean for the future of the Church? We're still figuring that out, but a forced reassessment for individuals and local churches across the board has been a positive development.

Especially because of the pandemic, that reassessment has led to a new style of church—"microchurches" and "house churches" where people feel more comfortable showing up and where more and more people are beginning to venture. Fresh Expressions, a parachurch organization that helps build these communities, has been growing.[4]

People are going completely off the traditional church script. My friend Paige runs an informal online church for NASCAR fans—many of whom are Christians who are less inclined toward traditional church.[5] Additionally, large congregations are forming minichurches within themselves, honing in on the important work of discipleship and relationship building that's been absent for too long.

The Difference a Church Community Makes

The reality is, you can find *people* anywhere, but there's something special about those you meet in a faith community. There's something you'll find at a local church that isn't present at a book club or a moms' meet-up or an art class. In the local church there exists a sacredness—a time and space set apart from the ordinary—that God honors, where He moves in extraordinary ways.

And though people have a knack for disappointing us,

it would be terrifying to attend church with a bunch of seemingly perfect individuals. How uncomfortable would that be? How uninviting and isolating.

Can you think of your deepest sins? It's not hard to bring them to mind. I don't know about you, but I want to commune with people who get what it feels like to be in that place. Church should be a healing place, not just a holy place. And how do we heal? Together.

I heard one pastor say that whenever a new person joins her church, she warns them that she's going to hurt or disappoint them at some point. They are free to leave, she tells them, if they are expecting otherwise. I kind of wish every pastor started out services that way. We sin. Not one of us is immune to it. But God's call is bigger than the failures of humanity.

We are a chosen people. We, God's people, are not atomized individuals but interconnected beings who need one another. The Bible makes it clear: This life on earth is about *us*, not just *me*.

As Emily Jensen and Laura Wifler write in the book *Risen Motherhood*,

God has given us many gracious outlets for relationship and community. These sometimes include like-minded peers, but his most comprehensive, beautiful, helpful, and hopeful design is a living body of believers. It's not just a group of arms (like-minded appendages that imitate the same things); it's a complex living organism where each person brings glory to God and love to others as they serve the head, who is Christ. . . . Find your flourishing, your *primary community*, in the local church.[6]

Do you need to go to church to have a relationship with God? No, you don't *need* to. But He tells us time and again in the Bible that He'd like you to be there. "Just as the body is one and has many members, and all the members of the body, though many, are one body, so it is with Christ," says the apostle Paul in 1 Corinthians 12:12 (ESV). God clearly grows our relationship with Him in the context of this ordained community of believers.

We are not supposed to navigate the choppy waters of heart, soul, life, death, and spirituality alone. Even if you have a good support system in a spouse or friend, faith is hindered without a larger circle of Christians to uphold us. Don't just take it from me; flip your Bible to page 1.

The importance of spiritual community has *always* been present. It existed before the first crack of light lit up the universe. God began with three: the Father, the Son, and the Holy Spirit—the eternal Trinity at the foundation of all of life. Creation teemed with lush natural beauty and communion between God and man, husband and wife. He created us to thrive on the presence of others and intends for our relationships with Him to be sculpted and enhanced by the people He's placed near us. That said, not everyone is wired to be among crowds all the time. God created introverts and the desire for meaningful solitude as well. It's all about finding the right balance for the personality type God gave you.

Nature most clearly illustrates how our humanity is more purposeful with one another. In forests, trees grow better when there is a mixture of species, their size and variety and complexity all snuggled up against one another, helping each other grow stronger, taller, and with more purpose.[7] The end result is a gorgeous ombré of green crowns overlapping one another, growing heavenward and more effectively letting in the right amount of light and life for the thriving of the trees and species beneath them.

As it is with nature, so it is with humanity. We need every variety of Christian, in every field, with every personality type—and we need them together for our personal growth and the ultimate beauty and purpose of the forest at large. You become a much more beautiful and helpful tree when you get your nourishment and enrichment from those around you.

Church isn't a building or an obligation—it's a refuge, salve, and fountain of wisdom and grace. If I'm struggling with a major decision or stressor, I don't skip church for weeks—I go as often as possible. Because even if God is everywhere and we don't need a building to find Him, it helps to seek Him in tangible ways, in places of respite where others can help carry us toward Him if it feels too hard to walk alone.

CHAPTER 5

Our Excuses

A MILLION GOOD REASONS

It can be very easy to justify putting our spiritual lives on the back burner in the face of urgent, daily issues. Many of those are true hardships that deserve a closer look, but let's put things in perspective. Most practicing Christians believe that having a strong relationship with God is important.[1] If this is true, why don't we make Him a bigger part of our lives? We often let superficial or less important things bar us from a more meaningful life in Jesus. There are several common reasons we women specifically don't prioritize going to church despite the inner call to personal revival.

Going Alone Is Hard

If you are single or married to a partner who is uninterested in church, going to a new church alone doesn't sound appealing. If you have kids, the challenge becomes even greater. Packing up the crew is a huge task. You'll bundle the kids up and find a seat—alone. Heading back or to a church for the first time can be really intimidating. Depending on how large the church is, you may not even be sure which doors to enter through or where the sanctuary is. Having a partner in little endeavors like this can ease the momentary anxiety, so if you don't, I get the hesitation.

It's not ideal to go to church alone. I wonder, however, if it would be worth the discomfort if it meant meaningful spiritual growth for you and your children?

The Holy Spirit calls people at different times through different measures. Maybe He will use you (in fact, I'm certain He will) to make an impact in the lives of those around you, including a partner who isn't ready to join you at church yet. God uses us as vessels of light for those nearby: family members, acquaintances, colleagues. In Matthew 5:14, Jesus tells us, "You are the light of the world." As a Christian, you have a beautiful opportunity to illuminate the darkness of the world simply by remaining in Christ. When you go to church, you are filled with more of that beautiful light and, in turn, can offer more to those around you.

My parents have been married for forty years, and outside of a few months here and there, my mom usually took us to church alone. From the earliest times I can remember, she packed us up every Sunday morning, rain or shine, and made sure we were in the building.

My mom also attended and brought us kids to small-group Bible study (where she studied and we played upstairs with other kids!) There were also church picnics and road trips, church camp and Christmas pageants. Even though Mom was usually on her own with us, we didn't miss out on the important parts of church life.

In fact, her independent, empowering spirit is an inheritance I appreciate more than nearly anything else she's given me. My mom never let my dad's choices or preferences keep her from doing what she knew was right for her children. In her bones, she knew that church community was important—and that knowledge was powerful enough to keep her pressing on.

When Work Takes Precedence

What if work is getting in the way? If a work schedule prohibits your freedom to attend church, that's a tough scenario. I have a friend who works weekends as a nurse and can rarely make it to something on Sunday morning. Her family found a church that offers Saturday-night services so church could happen for them.

The important thing to ask yourself is this: Are you meeting the need we all have for communion and closeness with God? If not, it's possible to seek and cultivate a path toward it in a local church. There are many people in your community who would love to help you find a space and time that works for you.

You may never find true spiritual satisfaction or know the depths God wants to take you to without these intentional action steps. Trust the process, and trust His Word to guide you there.

The Chaos Is Real

Then there's the chaos of life. Weekdays are a tornado—I know. Getting kids up and ready for day care or school is a gargantuan task that sometimes leaves me motionless in bed, unable to face the explosion of emotion that will soon erupt when I coax legs into pants, jam socks onto feet, and beg people to get their shoes on so we can get out the door. I'm making unkeepable promises to get my son to eat his Cheerios for breakfast and playing endless rounds of "The Gummy Bear Song" to keep the TV off and spirits high like *Groundhog Day* over here.

Afternoon pickups are capped by oft-rejected dinners, spastic rounds of wrestling, high-pitched screaming over whose Avengers toy is whose, and finally, an exhausted flop on the couch after five books, three songs, two hugs, and one prayer for two never-tired children. And that's just Monday. Hit repeat four times and somehow you make it to Saturday.

Saturdays can be great, but if you have children like mine, sleeping in isn't a thing, and there's always an argument to rise with the sun. Then we've got soccer and dance lessons, grocery shopping, birthday parties, and dinner dates. If you can only get to that glorious Sunday—when scheduled activity ceases—you *may* live to survive another week.

If you don't have kids, life is likely bustling with work, events, classes, volunteer work, and other obligations that mean a lot to you. You get up at the crack of dawn most days of the week and drift off attempting to compile tomorrow's to-do list in your head.

Such crazy life circumstances can make getting to church feel impossible. You may need to reevaluate ways to make it work and truly consider why it might be worth your time to do so. There are a lot more options now than there have ever been in the past. Many larger churches have multiple service times to choose from—times that don't require you to set an alarm or rush out of the house to beat the traffic. Other alterations (like skipping concerns about the right outfit and just heading in dressed as comfortably as possible) can eliminate morning stress as well.

Getting to Church When You Haven't Been Going

Going back to church after not attending for a while sounds, well, daunting. After years of reduced social activity thanks to COVID, it might even feel downright foreign. It's a place that requires "real" clothes, showing up on time, *and* some semblance of good behavior from children. Resistance to adding one more thing—especially one that may require vulnerability and effort—makes sense.

I would argue, however, that the Church offers something that other activities do not. In reality, most of the items on your calendar and to-do lists aren't spiritually satisfying. They are tiny straws used to sip out your energy and spirit little by little throughout the week. A vibrant church life can have the opposite effect. What if the effort you put into getting to church resulted in a more peaceful, connected, fulfilling life overall?

It *is* tough to get quiet amid loud circumstances, but once you know there's something missing, this fact is impossible to ignore.

Are the Excuses Good Enough for You?

A pastor I once heard explained the structure of our lives this way: Imagine you have a large vase. It is very wide at the bottom and gets increasingly narrow toward the top. The largest, most important pieces of your life must fit in the bottom, and there is only so much room as you move toward the top. Make a list of all the pieces you are cramming into your vase right now. Are the ones taking priority, holding up the rest, the most important ones? And are they really doing their job? What needs to increase and be shifted toward the bottom—the foundation of everything else? Do you need to rearrange your jar? Throw a few things out?

Take some time to really examine what you've got in there, to evaluate the purpose and value of each item. Grab a piece of paper and sketch it out. What are your buckets of busy? Could something be eliminated to make space for the life-giving benefits of a church community? Perhaps you don't feel like church or community is a "need" this very second. Often we don't feel like things are necessary until it's crunch time. But if we don't prepare in advance for that, they won't be there when it comes. Contemplation about these critical and foundational parts of life is well worth your time.

"Anyone who listens to my teaching and follows it is wise," says Jesus in Matthew 7:24-25 (NLT), "like a person who builds a house on solid rock. Though the rain comes in torrents and the floodwaters rise and the winds beat against that house, it won't collapse."

He then notes that those who don't follow His lead build their foundations on sand: "When the rains and floods come and the winds beat against that house, it will collapse with a mighty crash" (verse 27).

The question is this: What are you building your life on? We can hold on to our excuses for dear life, but what purpose do they serve? There comes a time to stop and take a hard look at our lives. It may be time to make some difficult decisions that will ultimately bring you to a place of greater peace.

If it's the deeper aspects of past church hurt or disillusionment hindering you, there's a lot to consider, and we'll do so in the next chapter.

CHAPTER 6

Our Pain

WHEN CHURCH HURT STILL HURTS

It's not just those who have left the Church who have been hurt by it. Many of us who still faithfully attend still feel the sting of past hurt. In order to remain active in church, we've had to look past the human error that deceivingly shaped the churches and leaders from our pasts in our minds. It's no easy task.

Instances of sexual abuse or misconduct and spiritual abuse immediately come to mind when we consider ways the Church has hurt individuals over the years. The Catholic Church scandals busted open in the early 2000s shined light on the devastating hurt that many people have experienced at the hands of church leaders. The evangelical world has experienced its own sex-abuse charges en masse as of late.

The denials, cover-ups, and inaction by church leaders have been agonizing to watch. After one victim, Jules Woodson, shared her story, she said this:

> We as a church, of all places, should be getting this
> right. . . . The Church should have been the first
> group to stand up and say, "We will not allow this."
> I want our churches to change how they handle
> sexual assault and sexual abuse in the church. It's
> a crime, not just a sexual sin.[1]

She's right. Some churches have succumbed to the ways of the world, fearful that public knowledge of such downfalls will taint the image of Christ. As if God can't stand up for Himself? As if saving face were more important than executing justice? God's character is *full* of justice—why would He not want that for His children on earth as in heaven? Again, human error is misrepresenting God's will for us. Although things are improving on some counts (as we've seen, more and more Christians are becoming eager to expose the truth), we still have a long way to go.

My own emotionally scarring experience in church culture serves as an example of overcoming. I can attest that God helped me see beyond the fallacies of past churches and into the holiness of His presence—but I had to work through it to get to where I am today.

In the mid-1990s, I was a middle school kid who had never kissed a boy. There are photos of me posing with friends after jumping into a mud pit and belly-streaking down a Slip 'N Slide at an annual festival designed exclusively to promote sexual purity. YouthFest was part Christian-music concert and part TED Talk, and it was focused on one message: Wait to have sex until you are married. I signed a "purity pledge" as a speaker booming in the background echoed the horrific consequences of sex outside of wedlock: pregnancy, AIDS, and, worst of all, becoming used and dirty for one's future spouse. The messages ricocheted around my mind for years, watering seeds of shame I was too distracted to notice at the time. The shame of sexuality enveloped me, and my relationships often ended in part because of it. I often became frozen, overpowered by fear of physical intimacy. I simply stopped being able to function. The purity messaging lodged so deeply in my psyche that it became like a disability. While the Bible focuses on purity of both heart (Matthew 5:8) and body, the Church zeroed in almost exclusively on purity of body. The messaging was confusing for many young Christians.

My husband has been a gift in helping me overcome this. He is a kind man with his own palpable brokenness who has allowed me the space to deal with my lingering issues honestly. He has modeled God's view of me by demonstrating that I am unconditionally loved regardless of my past and present circumstances or how fearful I've been. God has used him to help me seek truth and begin to find healing from the way things were messaged to me so many years ago.

Unfortunately, there are women who have had it far worse than I have. Rachael Denhollander, the Christian lawyer and mother of four who spearheaded the trial against USA Gymnastics sexual predator Dr. Larry Nassar, has a terrifying story of church betrayal. She was first sexually abused at age seven by a college student in a church she attended. The accusation was dismissed by that church at the time as they attempted to cover up the transgression.

Years later, when she spoke out about the abuse she had endured by Nassar as a young gymnast, the church she was attending dismissed her claims as well. Denhollander has worked fiercely to create a safe space for victims to speak out and justice to be served.

Despite the absence of her local church's support, Denhollander never felt like God had left her alone in the battle—and she never doubted the goodness of the Church at large. In fact, she actually *fought* for her local church, *fought* to stay in this specific community—even when they did not acknowledge her plight. Because she knew *Him*, she knew the church's actions were not *of* Him.

Rachael's story is documented in her book *What Is a Girl Worth?* In a podcast interview, I asked her what made her stay in the Church, what made her fight for something that had contributed to pain in her life.

"Ultimately, the answer to that is, I don't trust the Church—I trust Jesus. I don't find my security in a man-made church. I find my security in the body of Christ that God has fashioned and put together. Jesus is worth fighting for, so His Bride is worth fighting for," she said.[2]

That's the thing: The more you get to know God, the

easier it is to recognize what's part of His character and what's not. It's why we must move closer to and not further from God in times of trial. This is what ultimately transforms His Church for the better. Rachael is not alone in her fight for the Church and for her faith in the face of hurt.

Breanne's Story

Even when we know the truth—that God is not the source of pain inflicted by people—it still takes time to process that pain. If we can allow ourselves that margin to feel and unpack the trauma, significant positive shifts can occur.

It had been over a year since Breanne had uttered a prayer. She had become a Christian at sixteen and went to church faithfully for years, but things were different now. She was now in her late thirties, divorced and with four kids, and reeling from the hurt a longtime pastor had inflicted with his deep condemnation of the way her marriage had crumbled.

Breanne continued going to church post-divorce, hearing sermons that hammered the message *Divorce is wrong—one of the worst sins you could commit.* Her nondenominational megachurch didn't seem like the kind of place this might be so prevalent, but it was. The pastor she knew and loved conveyed an uncharacteristic disdain for her "failure." She decided to pour her heart out to him, confessing that his pointed remarks had stung deeply. He then told her that she had irrevocably harmed her children and that he was praying for marriage reconciliation.

"You start to think, *Am I ever going to be able to move*

on from this?" said Breanne. At this time, she had finally personally made peace with the breakup, and she and her ex-husband were navigating coparenting well by living near one another and keeping their kids in a familiar environment. She had been feeling refreshed in her faith after a period of turmoil. But the primary struggle, this judgment from her pastor, remained steadfast, and she began to waver, doubting the faith she'd once held so tightly. The pastor's words smelled of spiritual abuse.

Like so many who have experienced trauma, Breanne began to put up protective barriers. She couldn't help but reflect on the beginnings of her faith, when curiosity about God had led her to a local church youth group. She had been enthralled by Jesus, and when she met her future husband (a pastor's kid), that faith had strengthened as everything had fallen into place. It was shortly afterward, as a young mother, avid churchgoer, and volunteer, that Breanne had felt like her faith in God was the strongest it had ever been. But now, over a decade later, Breanne wonders how she's gotten to such a place of hurt and disillusionment. In low moments, it's easy to think that things may never feel different.

She hasn't let go, however. When obtaining her first solo mortgage was proving difficult, Breanne felt prompted to pray. As she recounts, she prayed,

> *God, I need You to help my unbelief. I need some kind of sign that You are there and are still invested in my life. I don't know how to find You. I need this to work;*

*I need a break. I need You to be the one to do it . . .
to do it in a way that it couldn't be anyone possibly
other than You. I need a sign, basically, and I don't
deserve one. So I'm just here, and I'm saying I need Your
presence and I need this to work.*

Within a few days, her realtor called with news about the
house—news that felt like an answered prayer. The process
moved along seamlessly, and she felt in her bones that God
was clearly reminding her He was still there.

Today, Breanne doesn't have the question of church
figured out. However, her past experiences with churches
outside the United States have left her feeling hopeful.
On mission trips to Latin America, the Church had felt
different—often, she said, because the experiences were
more personal. Partaking in Communion with sleeves of
saltines and juice boxes in the home of an overseas host
was "the most beautiful and meaningful" Eucharist she'd
experienced. This memory of consecrated sustenance tethers
her to what she knows in her soul is the truth of the gospel
message. It isn't Jesus she is rejecting.

"I like your Christ," reads a quote often attributed to
Ghandi. "I do not like your Christians. Your Christians are
so unlike your Christ." And perhaps that is how Breanne has
felt—or you've felt—over the years from time to time.

Breanne no longer feels abandoned by God—nor does
she blame Him for the past. She believes joining a church
is important and eventually wants to find a nonthreatening

environment where she can do so. She's opened her heart to the idea, a small step that cracks open the space for so much possibility.

If you have gone through something similar and memories of judgment are seared into your mind, you understand Breanne's emotional turmoil. Our minds and bodies, after all, are constantly working overtime to prevent physical or emotional pain. Who gave us that capacity? Our Creator, of course. Trusting in His embodied guidance to protect is a *good* thing.

Our Stories Matter

I often feel upset about what's happened at the hands of local churches. Churches where doubts, questions, or genuine sin struggles are silenced and shamed cause me great heartache. As a lover of Jesus and the Church, I want to fix it all. I've seen fundamentalist dogma create a lifetime of guilt for many, and we've all watched as spiritually abusive leaders have cultivated deep mistrust in authoritative church structures.

We can be assured that Jesus *knows* the pain you have felt. He was deeply hurt by religious leaders: condemned and targeted by them and ultimately betrayed by the people and murdered! If you are reading this, I can safely assume that you haven't been murdered, but Jesus was. And still, He believes the Church is worth fighting for.

When you think back on difficult places and spaces: You don't have to go there. You don't have to go down the road of fundamentalism or legalism or sexism or whatever it was that led you to this space of confusion or wandering.

You don't have to leave your faith behind to believe wholeheartedly that harmful past and current experiences are wrong. It's not "love it or leave it." It's grappling with it, knowing those actions are not of God, and working to change the toxic structures that have protected abusers. For that, we need you! I hope you'll remember this: "God has not given us a spirit of fear, but of power and of love and of a sound mind" (2 Timothy 1:7, NKJV).

Exposure of toxic systems and individuals is on the rise today. This demonstrates hope for a better, brighter, healthier local church. We're detoxing—and the exposure ultimately results in a greater glorification of God. There's never been a better time to rejoin or find a local body that is doing it well.

The world will try to drive you away from God and the Church. If you are looking outward for reasons to return, you may encounter the opposite. The world will tell you that you can be your *own* hero. It will that declare you are "enough" on your own. But there is no hero in this story except for God, who has given each of us the privilege of living and moving and breathing—for a brief period here and an eternity in heaven—for the glory of His name.

Standing on this side of spiritual hurt, it's tough to trust again—but God's Kingdom is upside down. As Jesus says in the New Testament, the way things are done are "not of this world" (John 18:36). We don't do what comes naturally;

we flip the script. Counterintuitive. Uncomfortable. Supernatural. That is the life of the Christian.

We can trust God to do just what He has promised to do—to restore and heal and forgive and rescue.

CHAPTER 7

Our Psychology

REPERCUSSIONS

Psychology is always a factor in a person's past hurt or trauma. It's important to think about how it may affect you as it relates to faith in this larger conversation. I was fascinated when I learned about the following concept from a psychotherapist friend of mine.

It is the idea of a *schema*. Simply put, "a schema is a cognitive framework or concept that helps organize and interpret information."[1] Although this can be great because it helps people shortcut through a massive amount of brain data, it can be harmful when it comes to traumatic events.

Mental frameworks used as shortcuts easily exclude new and important information. Because we rely so heavily on schemas, it is extremely difficult to retain new information about subjects we are familiar with, those things that don't conform to what we *think* we know. Thus, we can naturally revert to focusing on preexisting realities and beliefs even if they are no longer present or relevant. Still with me? Okay. As you can imagine, this can play a huge role in how we think about church when negative experiences from the past bloom easily in our minds.

For those hurt within church walls or by faith-based messaging, it can also be extremely difficult to redirect negative thinking patterns. One negative memory linked to a faith experience can wholly taint one's perspective of faith and church.

Consider it this way: A woman physically abused by her father may be fearful that all men are violent. In turn, she may spurn all males and refuse to commit to a relationship because, in her mind, all men are bad and abusive.

That kind of thinking can emerge in any circumstance where something negative has occurred. If someone experienced heartbreaking judgment or shame from a church in the past, they can come to believe that every church will treat them that way. It's a schema hard at work, living up to the American Psychological Association's definition that it "endures despite objective reality."[2] That's what happened to my friend Leah after growing up in a spiritually abusive church.

Leah's Story

From a young age, Leah was told that women don't matter, that they only exist to serve men and have babies. She grew up in a strict, religious home and in a church birthed by the leaders of a Christian fundamentalist sect she today classifies as a cult. It wasn't until years into adulthood that she heard someone say, "God loves you."

Between high school and adulthood, Leah came to question what she'd been taught about God her entire life, finally recognizing the sickness embedded in her religious background. "When you're in a cult, they don't tell you that you're in a cult," she deadpanned, speaking to me over the phone. "I never wanted to abandon my faith, but I couldn't tolerate the way I was being treated anymore."

Her faith crumbled for years when she first entered adulthood. Her schema was working overtime to protect her from another harmful religious experience.

But the seed of God's truth was planted deep inside her heart, eventually leading her to a faith community she could trust. It wasn't easy. Ultimately, she chose to attend church with a friend one day. She was skeptical and unsure of what she was walking into and whether it was a good idea. The church was a traditional Christian congregation, but the tone and teaching were strikingly different from what she'd known as a child. A woman was leading worship—something that never would have happened in the cult she grew up in—and that was enough to keep her interest. Still, fears from the past loomed, and anything that felt condemning quickly raised red flags in her mind.

She soon emailed the church leadership to ask some follow-up questions. It was in a meeting with the leaders, after she'd briefly disclosed her past, that a pastor gently informed her that she had suffered spiritual abuse as a child. He told her that they wanted to walk with her to pick up the pieces. And he wasn't just saying it—the church helped pay for Leah to get healthy spiritual and mental therapy to overcome her childhood trauma. It would take years of counseling, identifying triggers, and changing old thinking patterns before she fully trusted her new church, but eventually she felt safe. She overcame the powerful schema that had steered her in the past.

"As a woman, I had never been treated with kindness and respect in church before," she said. "And here these people were treating me like a real person." Today Leah is an active member of her church and a resource to those who have been through similar circumstances.

Psychologists work with patients regularly to rewire their schemas and approaches to various situations, helping them relate to their trauma with a renewed perspective.

In the example of an abused woman and in Leah's case, a therapist might work with her to help her see that not all men or all churches are abusive and, in fact, most are not. It would be a tragedy for someone who was abused to give up on all relationships or churches because her schema distorted reality.

Human failure, especially in the realm of faith and church, can feel connected to and representative of God. In reality, He is the angriest one in the room when His Word is twisted for evil. You are on the same team!

So why would we let *them* speak for *Him*? When I think of harmful teachers from *my* past, I can now clearly see their misrepresentation of the gospel, even if I couldn't then. After many years, Leah became able to see this too.

Everyone Has a Story

Even for those of us who didn't grow up in a systemically abusive church, it seems like we all have a story about a traumatic event from church that has been seared into our minds. One such incident stands out from my own life. On a youth-group adventure one night, the group traveled to a large house, down a secluded driveway, where a few candles were burning in the windows as the sun began to set. We were informed that it was a mock Judgment Day. We were to imagine that our lives had ended and we were approaching God for delivery of the news about our eternal fate.

A lump traveled from the bottom of my throat upward as all my crammed-down thoughts about death, heaven, and hell were unearthed from the far corners of my mind. I was directed into a darkened room where I saw a table with a Bible on it and a man standing behind it. He recited a verse: "If any man come to me, and hate not his father, and mother, and wife, and children, and brethren, and sisters, yea, and his own life also, he cannot be my disciple" (Luke 14:26, KJV).

I flashed to my parents' faces, tapping into the depth of my love for them. Hearing the verse read aloud caused a cold feeling to roll through my body. I could never hate my parents, but I also knew that I wanted to go to heaven. I knew the Judgment Day scene wasn't real, but I also knew that God knew my heart. "Are you willing to hate your parents in order to love God?" the man asked me.

My feet rooted to the floor, my teeth ground against one another, and my eyes stuck to the floor. I couldn't answer. The palpable reality of Judgment Day weighed on my soul. But how could I betray my parents by saying I hated them? And it would be a lie. The smoldering vision of hell loomed as heat rose to my cheeks.

"No," I said finally. "I don't hate my parents." It came out softly, but honestly. I couldn't help but imagine waves of fire embedded with sinners screaming, myself soon to be among them.

"I never knew you. Away from me, you evildoers!" the man quoted from Matthew 7:23, pointing toward a dark hallway symbolizing hell. I turned to head toward my chosen fate, traumatized by the vision.

After that, the memory goes blank. Given the post-event memory loss and detailed imprint of the scenario twenty-five years later, it's obvious that spiritual trauma was at work. I do believe in spiritual warfare, heaven, hell, and Judgment Day, but the way these things were presented was unbiblical, unthoughtful, and out of context. Scare tactics are never the way to share the Good News of Jesus.

I've overcome my bitterness about the past, but the experience lingered in my mind for years. These well-meaning leaders attempted to interpret biblical truth and got it really wrong. Perhaps they'd been steered astray by someone in *their* pasts. It took a lot of work for me to overcome this trauma. Acknowledging the way Scripture had been twisted was the first step. As I deepened my relationship with God, I realized that the God presented at the youth trip was nearly unrecognizable. Becoming more familiar with God's character helped me see how past narratives had been mistaken. This is why each of us must evaluate our pasts and make intentional choices about how we choose to engage with our faith differently now.

Being informed about how the brain works can make a big difference in the kinds of decisions we make moving forward. The church of your past, the church in the news— those are not the churches of your future. You can choose differently. You can overcome the past and discover a healthy future inside the faith God is calling you to.

Don't Be Imprisoned by Your Past

To the hurting: There's another option. There are thousands! There is no church utopia, and no earthly entity can live up to the Garden of Eden we crave and were meant for. But there are plenty of churches led by purehearted leaders pursuing God as best as they can.

As David Kinnaman and George Barna write in *Churchless*, "loving, genuine relationships are the only remaining currency"[3]—and that's all I'm advocating for. The institution (which is merely a shell) will fail, but the people (who are the true Church) and the God inside them are the value.

Sometimes I think we are considering church in all the

wrong ways. It hit me when I read something C. S. Lewis wrote about it. He said this: "The perfect church service would be one we were almost unaware of; our attention would have been on God."[4]

No sermon or program or promise offers enough for someone who has been hurt to return. But there are people— good ones, broken ones, forgiven ones—and there is God, drawing our attention toward Him and away from the soul-sucking pain of this temporary life.

CHAPTER 8

Our Messy Lives

FINDING GRACE WHEN WE NEED IT MOST

She was nervous to tell her small-group Bible study that she was unexpectedly pregnant, but Lisa was embraced with joy and open arms by the women she'd come to know and love in her church. Since she'd recently been divorced and had struggled through that emotional battle with her friends, she was afraid the pregnancy was an even more significant journey—with potentially worse social consequences.

But the moment they discovered she was expecting, her church rallied around Lisa, praying for her, holding a baby shower, and flooding her with gifts. When her daughter Audrey was born, the women in her small group arrived at the hospital to fawn over them both and ensure that Lisa was well stocked with food, supplies, and the breaks a new mom needs in those first months.

"I was nervous to tell people at church, but ultimately, they were my biggest supporters," she told me one day as we sipped coffee and watched our toddlers play together in my backyard.

Rather than feel outcast as one of the only single moms in the congregation, she felt loved and missed when she wasn't there. She was back at church with Audrey every week soon after her birth. Four years later, the two are a well-known pair in the children's ministry area.

Not every single mom has this kind of positive experience, of course. Studies show that 67 percent of single parents don't attend church or have the kind of supportive community Lisa encountered[1]—but things are changing. A few different organizations (Life of a Single Mom Ministries, PlusONE Parents, and even MOPS) have partnered with churches nationwide to start offering more programming and out-reach tailored to this specific group of women.

Perhaps not every church would have been as welcom-ing as Lisa's was, but many are. What helped make a differ-ence for Lisa was her participation in a small group—before, during, and after her divorce and pregnancy. If she had not previously been involved in close community or if she had vanished in embarrassment, she may never have received the love and support she needed. You might be surprised how much Christians want to be there for you when given the opportunity.

Lisa dealt with divorce and then single motherhood not in isolation but by reaching out to her church family. Her story exemplifies how Christians can support one another through difficult life circumstances with a posture of love and grace. Addiction, divorce, pregnancy, tragedy, job loss—name the ailment. A church family is meant to be a soft place to fall.

No Barriers to Entry

If a church is conducting itself in a manner worthy of Christ, there will be *no* barrier to entry—not a hint of classism or a whiff of superiority. As a young adult, I remember meeting a woman who was serving in the worship ministry at my church. One Sunday, she told her testimony of having previously been involved in an irresponsible, drug-infused lifestyle, one that had eventually led her to have multiple abortions. It had been years since she'd gotten sober, met Jesus, and allowed Him to change her life. Seeing her serving and speaking and representing His hope and forgiveness in tangible form was incredible. Just as God sees His people as fully forgiven through the lens of Jesus' atonement, so, too, can the Church when they welcome someone in.

When I was a kid, there were Sundays when my pastor would drop the sermon altogether and ask people to approach the mic and share whatever they might be struggling with. It was always spur-of-the-moment, God-led, and during brief openings in time when he knew people needed it. The atmosphere always shifted dramatically when we heard that the normal agenda was being swapped. On those days, we wouldn't be preached to by the pastor but spoken to by our fellow church members. There were enough repentance and release and healing and thanksgiving to go around. Open confession is necessary for real life and community to flourish and for God to heal us in our churches.

I know one woman in particular who found such healing inside a church. She'd grown up witnessing violence, drug use, and alcoholism and had become a mom as a teenager. When she began going to church in her early twenties with her daughter in tow, something supernatural began to take place. The pain of her past had become so tightly wound up inside her that she'd lost the ability to create relationships or offer forgiveness. The wounds from her childhood felt unbearably heavy. When she began an authentic relationship with Jesus inside the church, however, the load began to lighten. The light of freedom began to creep in. And although there are still repercussions from her past, she's been able to hold on to her relationship with the Lord and rest in the goodness and love of her church community. This creates a buffer of grace and allows her the margin she needs to process hard emotions when they arise and recognize that the past no longer defines who she is.

At one church event where people were sharing openly, a woman came up and admitted that she'd recently been suicidal. She was divorced and had struggled with extreme anxiety most of her life. She had struggled for years but continued to attend church on and off. In the end, her church family hadn't let her go, had continued loving and supporting her even though we weren't aware of how dire her emotional situation had become. The room was funeral silent as her voice caught, relaying the hopelessness she'd been feeling. But she hadn't given up—and each day of the past week had been a little better, she said. I wonder who else listening that day might have been about to give up but didn't because of her.

In these situations, my church leaders know well enough that we don't just need a sermon; we need a Savior. We don't just need a service; we need our stories. We don't just need Scripture; we need surrender. When we share our stories with one another, we're reminded that Jesus died for us all. We all carry silent shame, a hidden sin, a secret struggle. And we are all wretches requiring that amazing grace—from the nun in the convent to the pitiless murderer on death row. When it comes to equality, we've all got it on the sin scale.

If you ever get the feeling that you don't belong in church—that your mistakes are too shameful or that your lifestyle prohibits you from going there: It's a lie straight from hell. I literally believe that. God's grace covers every single wrongdoing and is vast enough to carry whatever you are weighted down with. There is no right way to be with God— He just wants you to be with Him, exactly as you are. If you've put your trust in Jesus, everything you've done or will ever do was forgiven before you were even born. It's done. He keeps no lists. He remembers no sin. You are insanely forgiven, seventy times seven times over. There's no catch—it's just free grace from God the Father. I go back to the scene of the Cross, where Jesus forgave the murderer who hung beside Him:

> Then one of the criminals who were hanged blasphemed Him, saying, "If You are the Christ, save Yourself and us."
>
> But the other, answering, rebuked him, saying, "Do you not even fear God, seeing you are under the same condemnation? And we indeed justly, for we receive the due reward of our deeds; but this Man has done nothing wrong." Then he said to Jesus, "Lord, remember me when You come into Your kingdom."
>
> And Jesus said to him, "Assuredly, I say to you, today you will be with Me in Paradise."
>
> LUKE 23:39-43, NKJV

This guy had probably never even been to a religious service, but had he been given the opportunity to get down off that cross after meeting Jesus, I'm guessing that he might have. With minutes left to live, he secured his place in the Kingdom.

As the Bible tells it, misfits and lawbreakers were the people Jesus liked to hang out with the most! We see Jesus befriending a Samaritan woman, someone Jews at the time would have regarded as a member of the lowest class of people. In this case, Jesus knew everything about her sinful past but still extended His offer of living water to her. Ultimately, this led to her sharing the gospel with the people of her town!

Jesus also saved the life of the woman caught in adultery,

and one of His dearest friends was Mary Magdalene, a woman who had previously been possessed by demons. Pretty much everyone in Jesus' crew was poor—they'd literally left their homes with the clothes on their backs to follow Him. They relied on charity for meals, housing, and protection as they traveled.

God also worked through many imperfect women we read about in the Old Testament. There was Rahab, a prostitute, and Abraham's wife, Sarah, who told her husband to sleep with her servant girl and then rejected the girl after she gave birth to Abraham's son. Still, Rahab played a major role in the Israelites' entrance into the Promised Land, and both of these women were upheld for great things in God's story.

Jesus makes it pretty clear who His preferred guests are in the parable of the banquet in Luke 14:15-24. In this story, an important man has invited a bunch of friends to his dinner party, but they are all too busy to make it. He soon demonstrates that such people aren't worth eating with if that's their attitude. He says to his servant, "Go out quickly into the streets and alleys of the town and bring in the poor, the crippled, the blind and the lame" (Luke 14:21). These, my friend, are the people Jesus wants to invite to His banquets: the humble, the grateful, the meek and forgiven.

As nineteenth-century Baptist preacher Charles Spurgeon wrote, "the most useful members of a church are usually those who would be doing harm if they were not doing good."[2]

I've met many people who fit that definition, those who

have been transformed by the saving grace of Jesus. He takes our vices and voices and transforms them into victory.

The entire Bible is pinned by a few key demographics—namely, the poor, widows, orphans, and the oppressed. Jesus is not interested in those who seem perfect. He's interested in those who are rejected, excluded, and struggling.

From Old Testament to New, God is very clear about judgment: It is His alone to make. The members of the special groups I mentioned above (poor, widowed, orphaned, and oppressed) are to be upheld, protected, loved, and provided for by the people of God. "The last will be first, and the first will be last," says Jesus in Matthew 20:16. Anyone who doesn't feel worthy to enter is moved to the front of the line.

I want to share a few verses that showcase God's prioritization of those who are struggling:

- "Seek justice. Defend the oppressed. Take up the cause of the fatherless; plead the case of the widow" (Isaiah 1:17).

- "'Defend the weak and the fatherless; uphold the cause of the poor and the oppressed. Rescue the weak and the needy; deliver them from the hand of the wicked'" (Psalm 82:3-4).

- "'The Spirit of the Lord is on me, because he has anointed me to proclaim good news to the poor. He has sent me to proclaim freedom for the prisoners and recovery of sight for the blind, to set the oppressed free'" (Luke 4:18).

As Christian women, wherever we may be in our personal lives, we have the beautiful privilege of being part of the Church *and* the incredible responsibility to help make it better for those coming behind us.

In the book of Acts, God says that we have been made "overseers, to care for the church of God, which he obtained with his own blood" (Acts 20:28, ESV). Jesus didn't die just for our individual sins and eternal life. He died also for *the Church*, these people whom we are called to stir up to "love and good works, not neglecting to meet together . . . encouraging one another" (Hebrews 10:24-25, ESV).

This spiritual togetherness is truly unique to the authentic Christian experience.

What Running Marathons Taught Me about Community

Years ago, I ran marathons—all 26.2 miles of them. The training was brutal. So many early-morning and weekend hours spent alone with my headphones and water vest, checking my watch every few minutes to see how many miles I'd clocked for the day so far.

At times, I trained with others—and what a relief it was on those mornings, slogging through a sweaty twenty-miler together. The first ten miles would fly by, with conversation turning quickly intimate in the artificial incubator of the run-space-time continuum. When we were running side by side, slogging through the hours, our chatter could get strangely confidential as we deconstructed broken hearts, childhood wounds, or the stress of daily life.

Marathon morning was electric, the fuse starting a day or two beforehand—a massive carnival of brand tents, apparel booths, gel samples, raffle prizes, and runners from across the country. We were kindred spirits ready to do battle together, whether on the concrete or the trails.

Arriving at the scene of a race, thousands of runners would be corralled together, bouncing up and down, stretching and chattering away in the cool morning air. There would often be the sound of DJs, radio announcers, speeches, the national anthem being sung, and special announcements about birthday racers or famous and elite runners participating.

Running alongside thousands of others and with cheering fans lined along the sidewalks for miles elevates the end goal of what's possible, marinating runners in determination to finish strong. Training runs are long forgotten as the mission at hand unfolds. Many will attest that crossing the finish line of a marathon is one of the proudest moments of their lives—a beautiful testament to the human spirit.

The impact of such an accomplishment, however, would be minimized were someone running alone across a finish line in an empty lot.

When it comes to this life, we can't do it without our people. *That* is a primary reason the Church exists. As believers, the community I just described is all the more important in the spiritual realm.

A marathon is bigger than an individual marathon runner,

and the Christian faith is bigger than an individual Christian. There's a larger story at play, one uniquely knitting God's people together for His purposes in the world and eternity. He made us this way on purpose, and you will not see the fullness of His promises for you here on earth lived out without the Church. If you have a desire to know God better or to see more godly fruit blossom in your life, know that it grows in the garden of the Church, in the company of His people.

CHAPTER 9

Our Complacency

WHEN WE FEEL SPIRITUALLY NUMB

There is another scenario that could explain what's plaguing you. Could the reason your faith feels frozen go beyond a typical experience of hurt? Restlessness and dissatisfaction—feeling numb from years of an emotionless pursuit of an inauthentic religion—have made some feel like pursuing a deeper faith is a fruitless endeavor. If this rings true for you, might the focus or purpose of your faith have been off target?

Let's consider it.

"A dead thing can go with the stream," wrote G. K. Chesterton, "but only a living thing can go against it."[1] When we are feeling numb or dead in spirit, we are easily pulled downstream with debris around us. The river seems out of control, and we feel directionless and destined for danger. Being dead weight and floating downstream is not a strategy.

What might spark the dwindling ember of faith inside you now? It'll take effort, but you can come alive and swim against the stream of disaffection. Many women today are in the market for revitalization. Can you do something different than you've ever done before? Can you rewrite the script of your faith story? Planted in infertile soil, growth is impossible. But you can uproot and transplant your soul into a place where springs don't run dry.

Emotions need not dictate our decisions. Like any close relationship, our bond with God is complex and wrought with history, context, and environment. The act of going to church without a deeper intent can turn you into a religious zombie. To attend church just to check the box or to revert to old, unhelpful habits devoid of true relationship would be pointless. Another C. S. Lewis quote is appropriate here:

> The Church exists for nothing else but to draw men into Christ. . . . If they are not doing that, all the cathedrals, clergy, missions, sermons, even the Bible itself, are simply a waste of time.[2]

Works-based faith can quickly lead to burnout. Church attendance alone won't cultivate a vibrant faith, but if you don't incorporate foundational practices like gathering together with other believers, spiritual fragmentation will occur. I love how Corrie ten Boom put it: "If you look at the world, you'll be distressed. If you look within, you'll be depressed. If you look at God, you'll be at rest."

Consider your relationship with Jesus and the Church in light of your other relationships. God gave us the marriage union and the parenting dynamic, for example, to showcase the ultimate relationship with Him. Neither one is a mirror image of it, but components that go into a successful marriage partnership or good parenting relationship symbolize aspects of our relationship with God.

Consistently practicing presence with God matters—in private, intimate moments as well as in gatherings with friends or family. Intentional conversation, disciplined sacrifice, and acknowledgment of a sacred relationship are vital because, as author Jen Wilkin puts it, "The heart cannot love what the mind does not know."[3]

Creating goals and intentions in your marriage and working to build up the union can be hard work. Similarly, a thriving faith will take intentionality and incorporate multiple components of relationship. A holistic faith is one in which all the primary parts are present. God gives us much guidance in terms of how we can live this out. Modeling ourselves after the way Jesus lived when He walked the earth is a great start. It's why so many Christians I know prefer to call themselves "Jesus followers." If we're doing this right, that's what we are.

Jesus interacted both with high-level political figures and with outcast lepers. He prayed among thousands and escaped into solitude for dark hours of communion with God beneath olive trees. He loved vulnerable children on busy days and cared for gossiped-about women in the wrong part of town. He prioritized close friendships with a small group and touched thousands with healing words of grace. He discipled a few, forgave many, and found rest in the Sabbath among His busy appointed days on earth.

Are we resting? Are we making time for people? Are we in prayer? In communion with others? Discipling and being discipled? Forgiving? Loving? Trusting? We can be assured that Jesus' life is our model, and it can be emulated in confidence.

Give and Take

Spiritual numbness may also be related to a consumerized Christian culture (sometimes called Christendom). The local church has often catered to this, offering entertaining bands, flashy stages, and diverse programming. When this comes without the core purpose of discipleship and growth at the forefront, things can go spiritually awry for members of a church community. There is nothing wrong with fun and entertainment, but a primarily consumer-driven church is toxic.

When we enter a community seeking merely to consume, the experience will ultimately be hollow. Churches that empower members to use their gifts to serve are the best kind to choose from. Contributing to the church body is part of how we benefit from our membership there. It is essential to spiritual growth and church health—and a healthy body of believers includes members who give as much as they receive. Practical tools like teachings and podcasts can be great, but we can't live off of someone else's spirituality. We've got to make our faith our own. Experiencing church as a consumer is like getting a sugar rush: It's good going down but gone almost immediately. We've got to do our own work—and that means evaluating priorities and making space for service and contribution.

I love how *The Message* paraphrases Jesus' words in Matthew 11:28-30:

> "Are you tired? Worn out? Burned out on religion? Come to me. Get away with me and you'll recover your life. I'll show you how to take a real rest. Walk with me and work with me—watch how I do it. Learn the unforced rhythms of grace. . . . Keep company with me and you'll learn to live freely and lightly."

"Burned out" (or "numbed out") clearly describes how many people feel daily regarding church and life in general—especially in the past couple of years. As the collective culture has navigated a worldwide pandemic, it's easy to see how the spiritual has slipped into oblivion. But our innate spiritual needs and desires didn't dissipate even if we ignore them. As beings created with a desire to know our Creator, we are always searching for more of Him. We see this desire reflected in many worldly spiritual practices, but none will compare to the authentic ones that link us directly to God the Father.

In recent days, there's been another deterrent for some: politics. We'll dive into that next.

CHAPTER 10

Our Politics

IS THIS A PROBLEM?

It's tough to escape the broader national conversation fusing religion and politics. Fierce political battles over religious liberty and demographic voting blocs partitioned by race and religious affiliation dominate election-season headlines. Even if you don't fit neatly into a particular group, the data draws an eye to the Church's influence over voters and forces some questions: How does our faith influence our choices inside the voting booth? And how does the Church mold and shape our political views?

Most of us are tired of people conflating religion and politics; we understand that decisions about these topics are personal. Unfortunately, the toxic pool of social media has pushed many people further from faith as politics has become increasingly virulent and intertwined with faith-based messaging on issues as wide-ranging as immigration, health care, and morality. The use of Americans' faith as a political pawn has been so off-putting.

The 2016 election year seemed to put faith in the spotlight like none before. As one woman put it, the experiences with friends and family "ground me into dust spiritually."[1] Many felt judged and jaded by those in a different location on the political spectrum. Said one woman, "I got called a white supremacist and a racist so I kept it to myself."[2]

Some Christians declare that by voting Republican, you aren't sufficiently loving your neighbor. Others judge Democrats who support candidates in favor of abortion and other things they see as wrong and destructive. These clashes often take place in congregations. Understandably, Christians on both sides of the political aisle have often felt turned off by such rhetoric. In such a polarizing climate, it's easy to feel judged, labeled, and misunderstood while attempting to vote in alignment with your values.

For Grace,[3] feeling pressured by her pastor to vote for a particular candidate zapped the holiness right out of the service on one Sunday in 2016. Ultimately, it led her to leave her church and seek a place that wasn't so overtly political. Grace ended up not attending church for several months, feeling alienated and torn about entering another space that might attempt to coerce her into voting a certain way. Eventually she was able to find a church that didn't do that, but the experience rocked her.

It's true: We don't attend church to get political lectures. But those who haven't been to church in years may get the impression that all churches are highly political. However, in my assessment, media sensationalism brews more controversy than there really is. Is political toxicity prevalent inside *most* church walls? My personal experience doesn't line up with the narrative that says that it is. I've never been urged by my church to vote for someone. After spending nearly twenty years as a legal voter attending church regularly, it seems odd to see stories of this popping up so frequently.

If you were watching the news and reading the newspapers in 2016 and 2020, you might have been convinced that it was normal for churches to hold campaign rallies and prayer vigils for their chosen candidate. While this may have happened minimally and under the radar (and more explicitly in select locations), churches that serve as political covers for politicians and policies are less common than you may think.

Pew Research Center has found that many churchgoers either don't know the political leanings of their pastoral staff (45 percent of those surveyed) or are led by a team of clergy that is a mix of both Republicans and Democrats (27 percent of those surveyed).[4] Just 1 percent of churchgoers said that their pastors spoke favorably of Donald Trump during the 2016 campaign. Only 6 percent said that their pastors spoke favorably of Hillary Clinton.[5]

The truth is that Christians span the political spectrum.[6] Some consider themselves conservative or right-leaning, and some identify as moderate or left-leaning.

You certainly don't need to have a certain political persuasion (or be interested in politics at all!) to embrace a deeper faith life.

Most churches have zero interest in playing political games with your heart or spirit. If you have struggled to reconcile your church or faith with political leanings (or lack thereof), I get it. I would not attend a church unless their clear priorities are loving God and loving others. If you smell a whiff of partisanship, feel free to depart.

If you do leave your current church or are currently searching for one, know that there is a movement of true, genuine, disciple-making churches blooming everywhere in this country. They are the ones who aren't dying out.

It's Time to Go Deeper

We *need* brothers and sisters in Christ in order to tackle the pandemonium that daily upends our world. Maybe for you the search for a deeper faith started with a terrorist attack, a natural disaster, or even the pandemic. It seems like everything has turned political these days, dividing families and communities across the spectrum. The years 2020 and 2021 specifically altered our reality like none other, plunging us into collective, long-term trauma with daily death tolls ticking upward on our screens.

Political tribalism doesn't help. You see death and destruction yet hear that more and more people are losing their faith, leaving their churches, feeling hopeless. It's no wonder that depression and anxiety have risen and suicide rates have skyrocketed. In our grief, we are collectively leaving our proven lifelines of faith and community behind.

And I know this: The enemy is sitting back and relaxing as we instigate our own doom. It's a self-destructive cycle. The worse we feel, the less we go to church. And the less we go to church, the worse we feel—as individuals and as a society. Satan exploits our personal pain, convincing us that eating the apple of enlightened, worldly knowledge will be the cure. He silently urges us to dismantle our faith, pushing the lie that God is the problem—and we are our own solutions. That's never true.

Let's return to the anchor that holds. Christians living in biblical community are the most powerful expression of God and the gospel on earth. You cannot go wrong when you pursue this divine vision. Ecclesiastes 4:12 says this: "Though one may be overpowered, two can defend themselves. A cord of three strands is not quickly broken." That's not just a good analogy; it's godly wisdom at its finest.

God *does* work through His Church. Paul writes in Romans 12:5, "In Christ we, though many, form one body, and each member belongs to all the others." The Church, imperfect as it is, is the vessel for His sovereign and supernatural work. Can we cast off the excuses that hold us back from participating in His heavenly revolution here on earth? Because you are reading this and listening to what God has put on your heart (to pursue Him again or for the first time), you are already part of something incredible He is doing. Check this out: Pastor and culture expert Mark Sayers writes,

"A study of history shows that it is precisely at moments like this—when the church appears to be sliding into unalterable decline, when culture is shaken by upheaval, when the world globalizes, opening up new frontiers and fostering chaos and change—that God moves again."[7]

God is moving now. Jump on board.

As author Lauren Chandler writes in her book *Steadfast Love*, "What we choose to use as our anchor determines how well we will weather the seasons of life."[8]

We need people like you, those uninterested in inauthenticity. Why let the grifters keep controlling the narrative? God hasn't changed, but the folks shouting the loudest have. God hasn't left the building—He's just behind the scenes, crafting what's next. If you call yourself a Christian, your presence is part of the game plan. He's had you in mind for this task for a long time: "He chose us in him before the foundation of the world" (Ephesians 1:4, ESV).

You don't need a church to be saved, but God *does* want you to experience the greatness of His Spirit in the communion of the saints (also known as the Church.)

I heard it said once that the easiest way Satan can destroy us is to get us alone. Remember that Philippians, the book of the Bible most known for joy, was written by Paul while he was chained up in prison. But he wasn't alone—he was chained beside his friend Silas, and the two banded together to praise and pray and worship. Their faith was doubly strong together and was therefore less easily broken.

PART TWO

Reasons to Reconsider

CHAPTER 11

Our Spirituality

THE MISSING PIECE

I recently spoke with a friend from high school, someone who considers herself "spiritual but not religious" and who has attended a variety of religious congregations over the years. Growing up, her Sunday mornings were for sleeping in, pancakes, *The New York Times*, and running errands. In high school, she began exploring faith for the first time. After trying out a Catholic church, she visited a nondenominational church with me.

"I remember that as being such an inviting, positive experience and feeling very moved by it," she said.

With these two religious experiences under her belt, she wanted to learn more, so she began a spiritual journey, attending a variety of services, trying to figure out where she belonged in the world of faith.

Now a psychotherapist who is interested in all manner of spiritual, mental, and emotional practices, her curiosity remains. It has led her to counsel patients toward church attendance in their battles to overcome depression and anxiety. She recognizes the positive effects of religion in forming vital connections for individuals and powerful foundations for a strong, interconnected society.

"There is an important place in our society for church. All the people I work with, all their mental-health struggles . . . so much of the problem is rooted in a sense of needing a purpose, community, and support. That hole can be filled through the Church, so I often encourage my clients to go to church," she told me in a conversation at a local Starbucks.

But she also acknowledged that it's very difficult "to go to a place where you know no one, where you've never been. And for someone who is already struggling with anxiety or depression, that huge leap is really hard."

I empathize with those who feel discomfort going somewhere new. Even a seasoned church girl like me feels out of place when visiting a new congregation. But if I were to move to a new city or be dealing with a deep struggle, the first thing I would do is find a place in God's house somewhere. It's an autopilot choice now because it has rarely failed me when put to the test.

Even while attending church regularly, I still deal with things like periodic anxiety and depression. When I let those things overtake my better instinct to gather with faithful friends, the spiritual fulfillment I rely on diminishes quickly.

Like skipping regular exercise or eating an unhealthy diet, ignoring our spiritual lives will ultimately come back to bite us. Yet, many American women are attempting to survive on spiritual junk food.

Dwight L. Moody once said that "church attendance is as vital to a disciple as a transfusion of rich, healthy blood to a sick man." When we are lacking spiritual health, we are sick. Consider someone who takes their vitamins daily, drinks plenty of water, exercises regularly, and gets enough sleep. Missing a few days here or there won't hurt, and overall, he or she is less prone to sickness and better able to fight off a virus and stay energized through tough seasons. The same is true of a person's spiritual life. The spiritual vitamins of prayer, Scripture, and church attendance keep us healthy and clear minded, connected and well.

Sometimes we don't even realize what we're missing until a change is made. I have a friend who once had to eat almost an entirely vegan diet for health reasons. Though she wasn't excited about it at first, her energy and gut health were so much better after the change that she never even considered going back to her old ways. The same thing could happen when we make changes to other parts of life.

We are all "sick" without God. Throughout the Scriptures, He continually emphasizes His Church and the importance it has in our lives, now and forever. In the Old Testament,

His Spirit dwelled in the Temple. Today, His Spirit isn't confined to a structure but is present in His people.

Some of us, particularly those in wealthier communities, may feel like our surface needs—those of friendship and support—are met. After all, statistics show that the wealthier the neighborhood, the more likely people are to be involved in their communities. That said, the day will come when our internal tanks are empty, when tragedy strikes, when short-term reserves aren't sufficient for us to ride out the storm. For that, we need a deeper well of purpose to draw from.

Illnesses, deaths, and other hardships always eventually arise. Those without a strong spiritual foundation buffered by a faith community may wish they'd built a support structure when the time comes that they need one.

Just as we plan for retirement by investing and saving years ahead of time, so, too, must we consider the importance of investing in our spiritual bank accounts. It's easier not to, but it's not wise. Now: Why is going to church so vital for that intentional investment?

This Is Your Life

I sat in the therapist's office tapping my foot, avoiding eye contact, and feeling fat. ("Fat is not a feeling" is one of the first lessons I learned that day.) She had just recommended that I enroll in an intensive outpatient program for women with eating disorders. I was nineteen and a college sophomore with a waitressing job that devoured my time. With a full class load, a busy job, and an extrovert's social agenda, I thought the idea of attending this program four days a week for six weeks sounded like a lot. Then there was the price—equal to half my tuition for the semester. I couldn't ask my parents to put down that kind of cash while also funding most of my college costs, and I certainly didn't have the money for it. I desperately wanted to find freedom from my eating disorder, but I was so busy . . . and poor. How would I cover my shifts? When would I study? What about going out with friends? *Plus*, I thought, *I'm not on the verge of death or suicide or having major physical-health issues.* My excuses could fill a whole spiral notebook.

This eating disorder had at first reared itself as anorexia, stripping my body down to a near-skeletal frame, and now had morphed into the never-boring variety of bulimia and binge eating. I'd gotten so thin that people had started whispering about me when I left the room. I'd dropkicked the rumors by gaining nearly fifty pounds in the course of a year when I couldn't control my starvation anymore. Eating disorders present the illusion of maintaining control, but they are actually master puppeteers.

"Can you put a value on your freedom? On your life?" she asked. In other words, *Isn't this program worth it to find your way out of this mental-health nightmare of a life?* Hearing the question posed that way changed the trajectory of my life.

This wasn't just my time. It wasn't just an expense. It was my *life*—my whole life. I was consumed by my eating disorder, constantly praying for help with it but failing to get it under control. I felt enslaved to my compulsions and disgusted with myself. I longed for something better, but it felt impossible to find. Yet here I was, rejecting the pathway to freedom. Because I was too busy. Because I had other priorities. But I knew that without this stronghold being rooted out, all those other things would be dimmed by the life-sucking cycle of my disorder.

I could struggle with this my whole life—or take a more dramatic step, one that required effort, discomfort, and sacrifice. It didn't take much more for my therapist to convince me.

I'm not alone in having felt this way. People battle physical addictions and mental-health struggles every day—going to therapists, taking medicines, practicing meditation, changing their diets—because these things have proven helpful in achieving freedom from vices and afflictions. Yet we rarely consider our spiritual selves in this light.

We are both spiritual and physical beings, the two parts cosmically intertwined, but we often live as if we're only the latter. The spirit enlivens the physical body; thus, that part of ourselves *must* be prioritized equally or more.

Spiritual things require spiritual methods. Our essence is in our spirit, which was created with an innate desire to connect with the Creator and our fellow humans. Our spiritual needs take action, care, and cultivation to meet. Prioritizing spiritual health and putting God first is the holy order our lives can best thrive in.

In *The Divine Conspiracy*, Dallas Willard explains it this way:

Seeing is no simple thing. . . . Often, a great deal of knowledge, experience, imagination, patience, and receptivity are required. Some people, it seems, are never able to see bacteria or cell structure through the microscope. But seeing is all the more difficult in spiritual things, where the objects, unlike bacteria or cells, *must be willing to be seen.*[1]

The spiritual is messy and confusing. There's not a formula for figuring it out. But we know it's there—and we must be willing to see it and wrestle with it.

Be willing to see, and blindness vanishes. We can facilitate this through our environment so we can better see and hear and feel God. He knows what is best for our lives—and He is asking you to live like you believe that's true.

Willard also writes that "the 'mind of the flesh' . . . is a living death. To it the heavens are closed."[2] Let us not close our minds—or hearts—to the heavens, which are merely hovering nearby, awaiting our choice to see God's glory in real time.

CHAPTER 12

Our Questions

THERE IS FREEDOM IN ASKING THEM

Nearly every night after dinner, I find myself cracking open the freezer to see if we have any ice cream left or sifting through shelves in the pantry for an Oreo sighting. My sweet tooth isn't exactly subtle. When I get these sugar cravings, I'm not actually hungry. I just want something to satisfy a nagging urge. Of course, after I down the Oreos or scrape out the last melted spoonful of ice cream, I feel tired or sugar-fried. In other words, not my best.

In a similar way, when we aren't searching for genuine spiritual nourishment (as I'm not seeking genuine bodily nourishment), we seek out what we know will taste good in the moment regardless of how long-lasting it will be. Such false sustenance is short-lived and packed with empty calories, just like my ice cream.

A nicely packaged quote graphic on Instagram or a five-minute sound bite on finding peace may satisfy us for the moment, but true nutrition for the soul is absent in these brief forays. We need more than pat answers and sermon snippets. We need rich conversations and substantive application of Scripture, prayer and trustworthy community.

When we're looking for something to fill us spiritually, we need good theology and context and grace. If we aren't building a toolbox that contains these things, however, they won't be there for us when we need them.

It makes sense that we aren't satisfied with simplistic responses or cliché comforts when reality stings. It makes sense that, at the end of the day, our deepest longings cannot be met by knowing our Enneagram number or reading the latest Brené Brown book.

We're deeper creatures than this! We have questions without easy answers, emotions without simple remedies. I know that for some people, presenting these questions and emotions in a church setting may have led you *away* from church. I often hear about people whose questions have been shamed, whose struggles have been reduced to thirty-second prayer requests, and whose doubts have been answered with a quick recommendation to "have faith." It's no wonder they haven't felt welcomed when they've received those kinds of responses to their vulnerability.

Such responses (or your questions in the first place) may

have kept you from pursuing a deeper relationship with God. In the past, I avoided questions about faith and science for fear that there would be no satisfactory answers. What I've discovered recently is that our questions—even the really sticky ones—are welcomed by and valuable and important to God. In a healthy church, they will be important to others as well.

Many others also have questions about faith and science. Studies show that this intersection leads a whole demographic of people away from faith. A brief foray into conversation about these two concepts, however, would reveal that some of the most brilliant scientists of all time have been and are devoted Christians. Many of the most important scientists and inventors in history were Jesus followers!

For example, Isaac Newton, one of the most famous scientists of all time, was a fervent believer in God and "wrote more about theology than physics," according to Rebecca McLaughlin in *Confronting Christianity*.[1] Michael Faraday, considered one of the greatest experimental scientists ever, was known as a devout Christian. Albert Einstein is said to have had a sign in his Princeton office that read, "Not everything that can be counted counts; not everything that counts can be counted."[2] These things may not answer all the questions, but they do show you that science and faith may not be quite as in conflict as one might think. This is just one example of how a topic you might be fearful of has more to offer than you realize when it comes to God.

God is in every question, detail, and doubt. He knows the struggles you are dealing with today. He expects your questions—and He's not angry about them. Truth be told, your curiosity *glorifies* Him! Proverbs 25:2-3 (ESV) says this:

> It is the glory of God to conceal things,
>   but the glory of kings is to search things out.
> As the heavens for height, and the earth for depth,
>   so the heart of kings is unsearchable.

How freeing is this? We glorify God when we marvel at His ways, which are unknowable to us. We won't ever have all the answers, but it is honoring to God to ask the questions.

Attempting to hash through them means something important: that you care about the truth. We need more people like that in the Church, not fewer! Truth, curiosity, and wrestling with questions in biblical community makes God happy. It's where we grow—among the other living things.

Giving Yourself Permission

A concept from the book *Overcoming Overeating*, which helped me conquer my eating disorder, applies here. The book specifically aims to rectify the binge/purge cycle of an eating disorder. I found the primary directive a bit odd: Eat whatever you want—as much of it as you want—for one week. No guilt or shame allowed. Talk about a scary concept: letting go of control and embracing the desire to overeat rather than pushing it away.

Little did I know that freedom was embedded in the

permission. When I realized I was allowed to eat what I wanted, I stopped feeling constricted by my food rules. This concept can also be seen through a faith lens.

When we allow ourselves to ask all the questions and wrestle with our doubts, we feel more freedom to know God—and open our hearts to hearing from Him.

If you can accept the state of your faith where it is, you can push off from where you are. There's no need to fulfill any quotas before reentering the Church. You are worthy to restart or re-up your relationship with God no matter where you are standing. Can you believe that God is going to meet you where you are—no matter how far away you are from the place you would like to be? God is okay with us amid our doubts, pain, fear, and weakness. Let your questions, curiosity, and faith drive you forward.

Children as the Example

The way a parent relates to their child serves as a good example of how God loves and accepts you in your current place. When my kids have big questions ("Mom, why do we have earlobes?" was a recent one), offer up incorrect conclusions ("The wall is white for us to draw on like paper, right?"), or misunderstand something (*Toilet paper is a toy meant for unrolling!*), I lovingly correct them.

If my child asks a tough question, I want to answer it as clearly and helpfully as possible. I want to help craft them into people of character and conviction, so I provide the very best guidance I can to make that happen. Like an adoring parent,

God wants us to become people of character and love. He wants us to hear His voice, know His laws, and strive to obey Him as best we can. He is gracious and kind and loves us unconditionally, just as we do our own children.

Like little ones just discovering echoes or rainfall or moonlight for the first time, so, too, are we in constant awe of the mysteries of God. I'm reminded of a hit song from years ago that says, "God of wonders beyond our galaxy, You are holy."[3] He is a God of wonders—the unexpected, the awesome, the inexplicable—and we are part of the big, beautiful story He's been telling since the beginning of time.

Don't Forget Your Value

This morning I sat at the kitchen table watching my five-year-old son eat his strawberry oatmeal. I was enchanted with the sprinkling of freckles across his nose and the way his periwinkle-blue eyes matched the shark on his sweatshirt; the crooked way the spoon was clamped into his sticky hand; the offbeat tempo of his feet knocking against the chair. I stared at him until he asked me why I was doing it. In that moment (and in all moments, really), I loved him so fiercely that it was pure joy just to savor that little face. My heart outside my body, just eating strawberry oatmeal like it was no big deal.

Now imagine that that's how God sees you. He's there to help you find everything you're looking for.

Going back to church to figure out some of these things is a great first step, but there may also be other things holding you back.

Worth the Work

If you aren't satisfied with the way past churches have grappled with your questions, find one that will hear you. There's no promise that it will be an easy search, but it is worth the time to find a community that will struggle through with you.

If you've ever given birth, for example, you may be able to relate to the deep satisfaction that comes with pushing through until you get something you've been seeking or waiting for. It's also an experience that, ideally, you wouldn't want to go through alone.

The process of labor and the waiting of pregnancy are incredibly difficult, but you know the reason behind the pain. And those laboring beside you are there to reassure you and talk you through it. Similarly, we know that laboring through questions and difficulties with others is worth the effort to find truth, beauty, and fulfillment in God.

As the apostle Paul writes,

We . . . groan inwardly as we wait eagerly for our
adoption to sonship, the redemption of our bodies.
For in this hope we were saved. But hope that is seen
is no hope at all. Who hopes for what they already
have? But if we hope for what we do not yet have,
we wait for it patiently.

In the same way, the Spirit helps us in our
weakness. We do not know what we ought to pray
for, but the Spirit himself intercedes for us through

wordless groans. And he who searches our hearts knows the mind of the Spirit, because the Spirit intercedes for God's people in accordance with the will of God.

ROMANS 8:23-27

The desire you feel to know God better is more than a labor pain. He's calling you to step into the process of transformation through community so that something great can come of it. You know the hope that exists within the process, but stepping into it can still be terrifying. Rest assured that the Spirit will intercede for you and the body of Christ will come alongside you if you have the faith to step into it.

As you diligently follow God's leading, you'll begin to know His still, small voice, His gentle guidance that comes through prayer, Scripture, and relationship. The more time we spend with God and His family, the more clearly we can hear His voice. There is no fast track to knowing God, so let's start building again on the foundation you may have started long ago or may be ready to start now for the first time.

CHAPTER 13

Our Discomfort

HOW IT LEADS TO GROWTH

Being uncomfortable is the worst. Why else do we often hear people uttering "Awkward!" in unsettling moments? Nobody dislikes the icky feeling of discomfort more than me.

But in life discomfort is often the key to personal growth.

In college, I was uncomfortable with the idea of completing the student teaching required to get my certification in secondary education. High school was only a few years behind me, and those faces in the classroom intimidated me so much that I nearly gave up the certification just to avoid having to do it.

"I think I'm going to quit the program," I admitted to

my dad on the phone while strolling aimlessly around Target one day.

"You're psyching yourself out," he said. "Just get yourself about five cups of coffee on the first day and walk in there as confident as you can be."

"Maybe," I said, as I envisioned stomping on my anxiety with my Payless heels, armored in an Express button-down shirt with a triple shot of espresso in hand. I wasn't convinced, but the conversation gave me enough fake ambition to keep my start date on the calendar.

It turns out "fake it till you make it" *can* actually work. Days later, I showed up at a high school lined with used pickup trucks and dotted with Carhartt jackets. Walking in went against every cell in my body, but I plodded one heavy step after another through the parking lot toward the front door.

After the initial introductions and first lesson, my nerves settled, my fear subsided, and I could admit it: It wasn't *that* bad. Within a few months, I clutched a double degree in secondary English education and journalism and was ready to take on the world.

I had a good laugh at myself later for the stress I'd endured about the whole situation, but the learning experience was invaluable. Even though I didn't ultimately pursue teaching as a profession, conquering my fear and getting uncomfortable was worth it. The fact that I hold on to this as a life lesson nearly twenty years later makes me grateful that a little discomfort didn't deter me.

When it comes to our spiritual lives, we may need to

become comfortable with a little discomfort if we are seeking any kind of spiritual growth. I know a few people who have faced their discomfort head on to advance their relationships with God because they knew they could be better.

Trading Denominations

Sarah Curran was raised in an evangelical megachurch outfitted with a booming auditorium studded with bulbous stage lights, a rotating rock band, and an advanced sound-tech crew running the show behind the scenes. It wasn't so much a church as a Christian wonderland cornered by info desks, prayer stations, youth rooms, and coffee bars. The essence of Christianity was diluted to its thinnest layer, a cheesecloth draped over the many initiatives percolating beneath the elevated, untouchable ceilings. You could find a friend from the gym checking people in or a fellow mom from school in the service with hands raised and eyes closed. But for Sarah, locating Jesus Himself was a little more difficult. Nothing she was experiencing at church felt like the authentic faith she aspired to have. Where many found their weekly dose of spiritual medicine, Sarah felt like she was ingesting a placebo.

"I'd be in church, surrounded by thousands of people singing and dancing and speaking in tongues, and I watched it like an anthropologist," she wrote in an email. "I thought it was all so fake; after all, how in the world could these people (always the same people) have holy experiences—like speaking in tongues, having hands laid on them, and so on—and then as soon as the service was over pack it all up and head to Cracker Barrel for Sunday brunch afterward like it was no big deal?"

She never felt at home in her faith in this kind of environment. She watched others parade their outward expressions of faith brazenly yet live no differently outside church walls than nonbelievers did. Friends chugging beer on Friday would sit piously in the pews on Sunday, wearing cross necklaces and proclaiming their faith renewed. God seemed like an accessory to a middle-class existence.

Eventually Sarah left the Church and went on a journey of her own, exploring ancient religions and dabbling in Gnosticism and mysticism and anything else she could get her hands on. She felt like there was something more, but it couldn't be found in the church of her youth.

Not everyone feels the need to fully understand the history and philosophy behind their faith, but Sarah did. Her quest led her to Catholicism, something she'd never even considered. But learning about Catholicism and taking the first step by going to Mass, a kind of service that is like ice to the fire of a nondenominational evangelical megachurch, was intimidating—and required her to work through backward stereotypes about a denomination that had often been demonized in her youth.

"What I blindly believed from my Protestant upbringing to be a backward and oppressive form of Christianity [Catholicism] turned out to inspire me and throw me back into my faith with all my energy," she wrote. "For the first time, having faith and reason actually made sense."

Now, living out a fulfilling spiritual life through her membership in the Catholic Church, Sarah has found a new home that has turned out to be not so scary after all.

Author, comedian, and podcast host Jen Fulwiler documented her conversion from atheism to Catholicism in her memoir *Something Other than God*, writing about how weird it was to repeat liturgy, do the sign of the cross, and mutter, "Peace be with you." Yet those very rituals were part of what ended up drawing her to God's Spirit in a way she'd never dreamed of. We may each be attracted to different iterations of the Christian faith, and God knows that! Give Him a chance to show you how well He really knows you.

Instead of looking at your search for the right church community begrudgingly, view it more as an adventure, welcoming curiosity about whatever God has for you.

A Dating Story

I discovered how to do this well back when I was single. In my twenties, dating was something I felt like I had to do but was uncomfortable. That said, I knew that it was one proactive way to find a partner. I hadn't done a lot of dating or had many boyfriends by that time, but once I hit the second half of the decade, I started to feel like I would never meet someone if I didn't put myself out there. *Sigh.* Wasn't this supposed to be organic? Wasn't God supposed to orchestrate this thing? It was against my nature to push for dates, but I skeptically entered the world of online dating.

First I just dipped my toe in by signing up for a free

thirty-day account on a dating site. Then I created a profile and began chatting with one man who signaled his interest. We chatted for weeks on end, but eventually we needed to meet in order to find out if this was ever going to be something more. Our first date was fine. I was nervous, but it was boring and he was unimpressive. I didn't feel a connection, but I wasn't sure if it would've been normal to feel one so early anyway, so I agreed to a second date. The second date went badly, and I cringed until the moment I could go home. That set me back a few months, but eventually I signed up for a different dating program and started to investigate again. I began chatting with a couple of new guys and decided that this time I didn't want to wait weeks to meet up. There would be a spark or not, and I'd rather find out right away than waste my time with false hope.

Suffice it to say that I had a few more failed attempts on the online circuit. However, I knew of so many couples who had met online that I felt like it was still possible for me.

A book I stumbled across changed everything. Essentially, the book's advice was to view dating less seriously. Rather than think of every first date as an opportunity to meet a potential spouse, the book urged me to consider it instead a curiosity-based experiment—in other words, to enjoy the company of someone new without expectations of it leading somewhere romantic. Everyone has *some* positive qualities, and even if you are not ultimately a match, you can still extract pleasure and learn something new from a date.

I soon began going out with more guys without

overthinking it and without letting discomfort get the best of me. I went out with five or six guys over the next few months, none of whom were a match but all of whom provided a decent evening chat. I started thinking of guys as humans made in God's image rather than grading them on the husband scale, which made dating far less stressful.

I began to recognize that just getting out of my comfort zone helped me learn more about what I wanted and what would be a good fit for me. It enhanced my discernment in my search for a partner, which is important. While I was searching, I still often felt frustrated and lonely, but giving myself the freedom to explore and be curious lifted the weight of wanting a perfect end result. This mental transformation would serve me well in the future.

This brief history of my dating life exemplifies how we can look at finding a new church or exploring a deeper side of our faith lives despite initial discomfort.

The United States has over 300,000 documented churches and even more that aren't documented.[1] God's house doesn't have to look one particular way, and yours needn't fit into a box. You can explore all kinds of churches with an open mind and healthy curiosity designed to help you discern the best fit for you and your family.

Expand the Possibilities

If a large congregation or building causes you anxiety or a specific denominational affiliation (Catholic, Lutheran, Baptist) rubs you the wrong way, get rid of the felt need to go that direction. Under the guidance of the Holy Spirit, this church-choosing experiment is *your* decision. Let's take back our autonomy like it's the twenty-first century, not the Middle Ages. Options abound!

One friend of mine had gone to the same church her whole life with her entire extended family. Therefore, there was ample pushback when she decided to change churches. She didn't know exactly what she was looking for but ultimately found a much smaller congregation, one that was quite different from the church of her youth. My friend is an introvert who suffers from social-anxiety issues as well as depression, so walking into a new building wasn't easy.

One week she was desperate, and she vulnerably wrote a prayer request on the church Facebook group. She was feeling empty and depressed, as if her life didn't matter anymore. She would later say that the flood of support she received online and in person was lifesaving.

Sometimes an entirely new setting is exactly what you need, especially if a church building of your past holds negative memories. Church groups now meet in homes and coffee shops and bars and gyms. These kinds of gatherings aren't as common as typical ones, but they exist. Just like kids with sensory issues who need to attend events when things are less busy than normal, some people have similar needs when it comes to church attendance. By identifying your needs and seeking out a place that helps meet them, you can cultivate a beautiful place of belonging in the Church.

A friend of mine and his wife head up a conglomerate of

house churches. Each one consists of anywhere from three to twenty people; the idea is to keep them small. When a group reaches a certain number of people, my friend breaks them apart. You can be in authentic community with only so many people, and this group believes in a church family that is genuinely communal and supportive. In smaller settings, things feel more intimate and trustworthy. This might be *more* uncomfortable initially, but eventually the quality emerges.

Getting Out of Our Comfort Zone

Never has the power of leaving my comfort zone been more palpable than during the weeks and months I've spent on short-term mission trips. In these settings, which emulate small church-group environments, God does incredible things.

As I once prepared to head to Africa, I envisioned myself being jolted through the savanna in a Jeep and catching sight of blue wildebeests, cheetahs, and families of slow-moving giraffes who were bobbing their heads to reach the leaves and twigs of wild apricot and mimosa trees.

Mozambique borders South Africa, Zimbabwe, Zambia, Eswatini, Malawi, Tanzania, and a 750-mile stretch of ocean to the island of Madagascar. The relics of colonialism live via the main spoken language, Portuguese. I spent the summer sleeping in a canary-yellow tent—a suffocating vinyl igloo—with a tentmate sleeping so close that our sleeping bags shared the same drops of dew that appeared each morning.

It was a summer of doing construction work with my team, binding brick-and-mortar structures that would house and serve the local orphanage. Side by side we used shovels to mix mortar into a sticky, gravely putty, and in the sun-scorched hours, we came to know one another well.

The memories and relationships from this setting are palpable—so many moments shared bonding over filth and hunger, beauty and need. The faces and stories I came to know that summer are unforgettable because my teammates and I relied on one another to get through—and *because* of the uncomfortable moments, like that first-day meeting when anxiety was high and doubts about the decision we'd all committed to loomed.

Not all of us are in seasons of life where we can go on short-term mission trips, but all of us can find ways to get out of our comfort zones and cultivate meaningful, memorable relationships and stories with people right where we are.

The Power of a Small Community

For some, the idea of joining a small community is terribly uncomfortable because in one there is no room to hide. However, tinier sanctuaries, smaller groups, and house churches may offer just the intimacy you crave. God can transform your spiritual life in the developing world or in a friend's living room. You just have to set foot inside.

Intimacy among believers is a huge part of the Church—a group of people who pour out their hearts divulging hardship, tragedy, joy, and pain. Vulnerability breeds thick in the safety of trusted relationships when superficial worries have space to dissipate. In the sobriety meetings I attend, we often assure one another that we are "holding space" for one another. Brain space, heart space, soul space, prayer space. We all need people to hold space for our wounds and for our joy.

Small, tight-knit communities like this can help move us closer to God and to finding healing in the sacred expanse of a gathering known as church. Sitting around a crackling fire pit beneath a black-velvet heaven studded with stars on a Saturday or cozied up on a creamy-white couch next to a roaring fire on a Wednesday—that's where you may finally be able to distinguish God's voice from the noise. These settings are the perfect incubator for the deepest parts of ourselves.

The Confessions We Make

"I was addicted to drugs for twenty years, but my wife stuck with me," said one man I knew in a small group.

Prior to this gathering, he'd been getting on my nerves. He talked too much and mentioned his wife, Twila, in every other sentence. He was *too* positive and excited for every meeting to get started.

But that night he shared how he'd found Jesus and changed his entire life in an instant—stopped the drinking and drugs cold turkey and never looked back. His positivity came as an aftereffect of the new lease on life he'd found—a life that prior to this transformation had been mostly dark. He'd spent part of it in a jail cell contemplating suicide. Yikes. I felt my prior judgment melt away.

He didn't get on my nerves much after that. After hearing his story, I viewed him with reverence and respect, sort of awed by how he'd climbed out of a hole deeper than I'd even dreamed of looking down. It's in these slow, quiet moments that we can actually hear someone and, in turn, begin to feel safe enough to share parts of ourselves. It's perhaps where God does His best work.

One woman in my small group had been attending our church for some time. She was originally from China and spoke very little during our group. I initially got the impression that she was unfriendly. I had a hard time getting to know her—until her story changed everything.

She had grown up in a pagan household, and a Christian friend had shared Jesus with her. She'd soon begun attending a house church, but her parents didn't approve of her new faith. They gave her an ultimatum: Give up Christianity or give up her family. She chose Jesus, and her family disowned her. That was several years back, and she hadn't spoken to them since. She had given up everything for Jesus, just as the apostles had done and just as He calls us to in the Gospels. I had been asked to do so little in comparison. Suddenly I felt like I was on mission with a princess warrior.

In another small-group setting, a married couple joined us on a trip we all took together, leaving their one-year-old daughter at home with her grandparents. The wife was verbose and confident while her husband was quiet and devoted. Five days into the trip, their marital troubles surfaced. Tears and tension invaded our group as we sat cross-legged on the concrete floor or sank back on elbows against shoddy picnic tables. We heard "divorce" uttered as the woman expressed what they were going through, a difficult piece of their life that hadn't had room to breathe back home. Something about the group, the space away from everyday life, gave the hardship room to be wrestled with.

Here, in an outdoor shelter lit only by flashlights, the grit found its way to the surface. There were no helpful platitudes. There wasn't a neat little Bible verse to calm the very real troubles in this couple's relationship. But there was honesty. There was space for hurt to brood and words to be spoken. A year later, I ran into them. They had worked through the issues and were happy, with another baby on the way. I like to think that being able to hack away at their problems honestly among loving Christian friends played a part in that. There was a place for questions and lament and fear among newly trusted friends. It was uncomfortable, but it was holy and good.

CHAPTER 14

Our Loneliness

COMBATING THE EPIDEMIC

Since the advent of the Internet, connections online have become legion, but interpersonal relationships seem to have dissipated. We've become superficially overconnected and authentically underconnected. There are certainly genuine, meaningful relationships formed online—like friendships forged over hobby blogs and writing groups, Instagram interests and Facebook pages. But by and large, avatars and comments sections have too often replaced lunch dates and movie nights with friends (among other traditional in-person gatherings). Many of us now work from home, communicating with coworkers exclusively via Zoom, order and receive groceries to our doorsteps via apps, and stream random sermons to our cell phones.

Even answering the phone to speak voice to voice is uncommon now: Calls have been replaced by rounds of texts, and social-media memes joke that millennials and Gen Zers are horrified if their phones actually ring. Sadly, communicating via texts and emojis lacks the human empathy and honesty that a caring tone can convey. It also makes it very easy for someone to struggle in isolation, covering up their hardship with the right responses, smiley faces, and exclamation points.

As use of the Internet has skyrocketed, rates of depression have risen significantly among Christians and non-Christians alike.[1] It strikes me that when it comes to mental health, depression has always been more prevalent in women than in men (even apart from our high proclivity for postpartum depression, which can last for years). Every year at least twelve million women experience depression,[2] and rates have tripled across the entire population since the pandemic began in 2020.[3]

It's quite common for women to feel lonely in their adult lives. (Despite many of us believing that marriage will solve the problem, it doesn't.) These days it's common to live far away from extended family. Since people are getting married later, it's easy for singleness to become a weight of isolation. Many stay-at-home moms feel the struggle of loneliness as they spend days at a time without any real adult community outside of nightly conversations with their husbands.

It's no coincidence that rates of church attendance and departure from faith line up with more Internet use and more depression. These integrated factors create the perfect storm. One little-known piece of emergent data surprises me: After one year of the pandemic, those who attended church weekly (in-person or online) during that time reported higher levels of mental health than those who attended less frequently or not at all.[4] Even people who went sporadically to church scored lower. There is something about the regular rhythm of church community that contributes to spiritual and mental health in a way nothing else does.

In his book *Lost Connections*, Johann Hari found that "Depression is—in fact—to a significant degree a problem not with your brain, *but with your life*."[5] He discovered that a person's circumstances and environment are far more predictive of whether they have depression than their brain chemistry is. For example, "In rural Spain, depression was extremely low— because there was a strong community protecting people."[6] We don't always automatically have that kind of strong community, but we can create one in a church family. You see tight-knit, happy communities in the Mormon population in Utah and among the Amish in various parts of the country. Could we replicate some of their family-style spirituality?

The word *community* can at times be overused in conversations related to mental health—but it can't be replaced. Whether a person is religious or not, healthy community matters for everyone for a whole host of proven reasons. Research proves that community is essential to good mental health.[7] Hari famously wrote that "the opposite of addiction . . . is human connection."[8] It makes all the difference. And the Church is one of the only open communities, barrier-free and available to people of every color, creed, sexuality, and socioeconomic background.

Mental-Health Benefits

One eye-opening study found that American women who attend religious services at least once a week are five times less likely to commit suicide than those who don't.[9] In fact, there's plenty of strong evidence that people who attend a church or synagogue regularly are less inclined to take their own lives than other people are. That is some powerful information, but it's not often circulated widely.

Forty-five thousand Americans take their own lives each year, and twenty-five times as many attempt to. Every year, institutions and organizations devoted to reducing the toll of suicide in America's communities publish resources devoted to prevention. Some of the most prominent ones come from the National Suicide Prevention Lifeline and the American Foundation for Suicide Prevention. Yet attending religious services isn't included on these lists of resources. Why? It doesn't make sense.

Data isn't sexy, but it sure tells us a lot. More of it reveals that those who regularly attend church are happier and less anxious than those who don't.[10] This is not to say that church-going Christians don't suffer from depression or mental illness; I would never want to convey that church attendance is a magical cure. Therapy, medication, and strong relationships are also vital parts of staying mentally healthy. And sometimes a mental illness—because it is an illness—overpowers every other factor.

But the numbers don't lie: A church community does contribute to better mental well-being. Talk about holistic self-care! This is part of it—and it'll be there as a buffer when life hands you (or others) a lemon. Trusting this fascinating data about the simple act of attending religious services is a quintessential way to love our neighbors and ourselves well.

Consider this: If you aren't going to church regularly, it's very unlikely you'll develop the habit of doing it when life gets more difficult. But if you have a regular spot and end up in the pews out of habit, God can meet you there, where you've subconsciously opened your heart up for healing. In moments of darkness, we often don't know what we need until God provides it. I don't know about you, but I want to unveil every opportunity possible to receive that in those times. Create the best opportunity for God to move in your heart by showing up at His door every week.

Something is telling you not to abandon this part of your life any further. Your scope of experience—both in the world and as a spiritual being—is tiny. Are you ready to believe there's a whole lot more to be revealed? We haven't experienced a fraction of the goodness of God just yet. Can you trust that He wants to show you something more? "Draw near to God and He will draw near to you," says James 4:8 (NKJV).

Isn't that exactly what you're doing right this second? He's drawing near to you *right back*. Keep going.

The Reason You Are Drawn to the Church

It's always been this way: Human nature is that we are drawn to warm bodies and kindred spirits. So it was with the very first church in the Garden, where the triune God gathered with two humans, Adam and Eve, who experienced perfect worship and communion.

This vision continues throughout the Bible. Jesus intentionally traveled in groups, addressing gatherings, reading Scripture, and laying the foundation of the Church for us. The Bible is written to churches, groups of people, not exclusively to individuals. God makes it very apparent: His desire is for us to gather and worship and study His words as a people.

We will always feel a spiritual ache for more when we aren't part of a local church. The imprint of God on our souls cultivates in us the desire to be close to others and generates compassion and generosity toward humanity. We were created for a very specific, special, and sanctified kind of community. Without it, each of us is a missing appendage floating in spiritual space and unable to be fully grounded or known.

Being Part of Something Bigger

Since most people aren't living with built-in community today, seeking it out on your own is essential. What would it look like to engage and be part of positive change in the local church? To do so would be a benefit to yourself, your neighbor, your community, our society, and humanity. Church people have a radiating effect on the flourishing of every aspect of the world. That's exactly how God created it to be! His Church, the Christians He has called to bring the Good News to the world, works in tandem and unity to cultivate light, life, hope, and goodness wherever we are.

Being part of the local church is *directly* related to loving your neighbor. It's through this entity that we see needs, hear vulnerability, and have opportunities to serve the community plopped in our laps. We are busy. We are women—working, cooking, doing yoga, surviving—and the needs of others are hard to see through the fog of our own needy lives. The Church draws us out of that fog and into the larger story of God's work in His world and in the lives of those around us.

We belong there, and we will be used by God to enhance the world for Him when that's where we are. The Bible tells us that we are the light of the world—but we are brighter together! We are not meant to be alone.

Though the ultimate cravings we have for spiritual fulfillment cannot fully be met on earth, the Church is the closest place to heaven we will find here.

CHAPTER 15

Our People

WHAT HAPPENS WHEN WE GATHER

Throughout the course of my life, I've gone to church while on every point of the emotional spectrum: empty, scared, and alone—and happy, victorious, and content. I've gone in good times and bad—in the midst of personal faith highs and in the lows of my worst, unmentionable sins. I've gone hungover and miserable. I've gone joyful and on the eve of life-changing trips overseas and other places with my church family where I would be changed forever.

I've joined a dozen small groups—some awful, some fantastic—and found lasting friendships with incredible women. Meanwhile, I've experienced the depths of depression, heartbreak, insecurity, and moral conundrums, and I've been in the lowest valley of an eating disorder—one I journeyed through for over a decade.

I've been to church everywhere: beneath the leaves of Kenyan Maasai Mara trees, their dry, evergreen branches shading me from a spicy, equatorial sun rising from the east; in Venezuela, where the church was a large, tin-roofed structure with sunlight pouring in the side windows and heat that you could eat in pieces around you—nearly suffocating. But the Venezuelans were used to it, and for a few moments I forgot the sweat inching down my earlobes and remembered the simple words we'd practiced: *Estoy alegre*—"I'm happy." In both of these instances, no one around me spoke English, but I felt a beautiful kinship with my brothers and sisters in Christ because we were at church together.

There was the gospel-brunch church service I attended in downtown Los Angeles, and the time I sat on sand-infused pews in a church on Sanibel Island, Florida. I've been to a Catholic Mass in Washington, DC, and a traditional Pentecostal worship service in rural Indiana—and in each place I've met God no matter how much I've enjoyed the atmosphere or the company around me. And while there have been plenty of mornings I haven't felt like going to church, I've never regretted showing up.

Outside church walls, the presence of Christian brothers and sisters has also provided comfort. On one youthful adventure, I entered the host home I was staying at in Bangalore, India. I'd just completed a twenty-four-hour journey across the globe and was terrified in the 2:00 a.m.

darkness as I rode silently in a rickshaw with an older couple who said little to me during the thirty-minute trip. When we finally arrived at their home, I spotted an image of Jesus framed on the wall. Immediately my anxiety felt a tug of release. I felt, in some small way, like we were gathered—the three of us who loved Jesus—and that meant that God was there.

These were profound moments when I recognized that I could go anywhere in the world but step into a church and know that God was there. While not every church is healthy or safe, many are, and I can attest to the security and love I have felt in my own. That is the Holy Spirit working, bringing God's beloved together as one in every circumstance, in any place the two or three or thousands might gather.

While two or three gathering is great, it's often in corporate praise and worship that God shows up most powerfully. I can walk into church utterly resistant, unhappy to be there, with a headache spiking and doubts lurking, but the moment voices lift in praise, it's like we all momentarily let go of the baggage that consumes our lives. It's like a little preview of heaven, where everything is already good, where the Spirit infiltrates the pews, the chairs, the couches, the floor—whatever we happen to be sitting or standing on. Differences cease; languages convene; love and worship overwhelm insecurity, doubt, and fear; for just a bit, we remember exactly who made us and why we have been made at all—to worship our Creator.

I'm often reduced to joyful tears in these settings,

overwhelmed at the unconditional love of the Father, who shows up in powerful ways when we sing to Him. It's a love beautiful enough to make me believe that if I just show up at the service, God is going to be there.

These kinds of experiences are happening around the world every week, in new and old churches alike. They needn't look the same to honor God. Some people understand the Church as a collection of nouns: pews and screens, pastors and parking lots, youth groups and Sunday school classes. But those things are merely accessories. What is the Church *really*? A communion of broken souls fused together placing their hope in something greater than themselves alone.

When God Uses the Church to Free You

Even though I've had many friends in my life, there used to be one thing I felt unsafe talking to almost anyone about. It was going to take a certain type of community for me to air my grievance, and it ended up taking two years of building trust within my church space for me to do so. Now I can tell you because I told them and was able to break the chains of shame.

For many years, I struggled with my relationship with alcohol. To be honest, it's still a struggle—at least as I'm writing this today. I never had a physical addiction, but the mental stronghold was brutal. Well into my thirties, I finally began to question if I could ever overcome the way this substance seemed to hold power over me. I wasn't ruining my life, hurting my children, losing my job, or hitting some kind of rock bottom. But I felt controlled by a substance that was always calling me back to it with promises of relief; it was a fast-numbing brain balm I could use to shade-block reality.

I often flashed back to shameful nights of drinking when I was younger—what some might call normal partying during the college and post-college years. Unfortunately, I had embarrassed myself and been in dangerous situations more times than I could count. I had occasionally blacked out and didn't have the guts to ask anyone what had happened in those lost moments. My partying days were far behind me by the time I was questioning my ability to give up alcohol. But I couldn't help but fear that one day I could accidentally do something stupid again—and this time, it *would* ruin my life.

Because alcohol is so culturally pervasive and celebrated, it's socially disrupting and uncomfortable to mention that you might have a hard time with it. Wine is a common solution offered in jest (or seriousness) for all things #MomLife. Not everyone has difficulty with alcohol, and for some it truly can be a way to relax in a mentally healthy way at the end of the day. But not for me.

Regardless, I kept quiet about my concern for years, even when a night out with friends would result in a life-sucking hangover or when I would wake up in the middle of the night after drinking a bottle of wine with a headache and regret paving the way to another promise to myself to quit. The regretful nights were few and far between, but two glasses of wine a night was par for the course. It wasn't something I could take or leave—it was an itching in my mind that needed to be scratched and left me unsatisfied and longing if it wasn't. I also had rules: No liquor, because I was apt to sneak a long chug of ice-cold vodka in a tough moment if it was stashed in the freezer. No drinking on Mondays. No drinking on an empty stomach. The rules felt like boundaries, but they were bars.

It all felt so similar to the eating disorder I'd overcome years before, like I was using a coping mechanism to get by but feeling jailed by its power over me. It wasn't until I rallied the courage to share with my small group what I was struggling with—and that I wanted to quit drinking—that I began to break free.

With my voice shaking, a lump in my throat, and heat beating my cheeks, I admitted my problem—let it breathe the air of truth for the first time. Oxygen kills secrets.

What would they think of me? Here I was, this church-going mom who wrote about God and professed to love Him, yet I was struggling with this secret addiction. Would they think me a bad mom? A bad Christian? I worried that I'd be judged if I ever picked up a drink again. It was one of the most vulnerable moments of my life to confess my struggle to the girls—but it soon transformed into the most freeing. "Shame loses power when it is spoken," says Brené Brown[1]—and let me tell you how true that is.

The confession launched me into a long period of sobriety and eliminated the fear of sharing openly almost immediately. It's still slightly unnerving to write about it in this book, and I never could have done it back then, before I silenced the shame with words and community. Today I'm nearly two years sober—and I couldn't have gotten here without the unconditional love and trust I found in that small group of church friends and the strength of the awesome God within me.

I have no problem with attending secular events and hanging out in non-Christian groups, but as a Christian I need a community where the support and vulnerability are rooted in Christ. Currently I regularly attend nonreligious online support meetings, and I love them, but they often ring hollow in the hardest moments. There's a lot of self-love and support there, which can be great, but I also need to be surrounded by folks who know my heart for the Lord and can uphold me with Scripture and His promises when those of the world don't cut it.

I need Jesus to be the center and everything else to grow around Him. Too many times, I see well-meaning programs and activities making self the center—and ultimately this is a dead end. We can personalize nonreligious support meetings to be in alignment with our faith, but it's necessary to acknowledge that they are an extra add-on and don't take the place of Christ-centered community, to which we are called.

Alcoholics Anonymous is actually a great model for getting the most out of community. Spend any time among the addicted, those trying and failing and trying again to stomp out their personal demons, and things get holy pretty quickly. In AA meetings (often held in church basements, ironically enough), people find the family, support, and structure they desperately need—bringing the empty vessels of their lives to the table and asking those around them to help fill them up. And they do.

Façades and charades do not exist in the recovery community. They shouldn't exist at church either. When they don't, it brings about the kind of honesty and vulnerability that breaks the seal between heaven and earth, soul and skin. But you shouldn't have to be addicted to alcohol or drugs to find a safe space. And you don't have to be. That's part of why I'm writing this book—to let you know that there's a church where your shame and secrets and sin are safe to share.

Just like an AA meeting, church is awkward and bruised and stained with grape juice or coffee. It's inconvenient and humbling, patience building and soul vexing. But it's teeming with real life—and God is there at the core of it.

If you feel the pull to draw closer to God, walk forward. If you're worried that the Church won't have what you're looking for, keep reading. God has a community for you. It might take a little legwork, but the benefits of a deeper, stronger relationship with God and others are worth the search. What I've learned about how our personal lives and the world at large are affected by simply getting back to church, one person at a time, is fascinating.

Have People Stopped Gathering These Days?

There are other reasons why spiritual gathering matters. Before the pandemic, I began reading about how people were leaving the Church. It was concerning—not because church attendance means that you're a "real" Christian but because drifting from the Church means that the faith and the Christian values that shape society and our lives are being diminished. This has all kinds of unforeseen consequences. When we as believers stop gathering as the Church, the values that so many of us hold dear—service, justice, love, and compassion—become more and more disconnected from the One who created them.

Thankfully, when I dug a little deeper, I discovered a different truth: that the vast majority of people believe in God and desire a closer relationship with Him, whether or not they are attending church.[2] Sometimes it's harder to do something when it feels like you are alone, but you can be confident you aren't alone in this. There are many women on this journey, unsure how to get where they are going. It's why I wanted to write this book and create a community where we can find our way together.

I know many people are looking for a way back yet are unsure of the path. There is no blueprint. Along with praying for the journey, educating and empowering ourselves to make wise, informed choices is the best thing we can do—and you are doing it.

CHAPTER 16

Our Presence

SHOWING UP IS POWERFUL

You know by now that the Church—the gathering of God's people—is the foundation on which a strong spiritual life is built. Ephesians 5:29 reveals that the Church is God's physical body on earth: "No one ever hated his own flesh, but nourishes and cherishes it, just as Christ does the church" (ESV).

God tells us very clearly that it's impossible to know Him well without participating—being present—in holy times of *ekklēsia*. Sometimes it can feel like we have a close relationship with God, but it's tough to analyze the truth of that without something to compare it to. Couldn't it be better, closer, deeper?

Maybe it seems difficult to believe that something as ordinary as going to church could be vital. After all, you may find a lot of people there you wouldn't naturally gravitate toward. But that is the beautiful thing: We know that God has specifically ordained them to be our brothers and sisters in Christ at this particular moment in time. It's our job to be present and available to participate in this work He is doing among believers.

When the Holy Spirit is involved, anything can turn into revival. The love we eventually develop for our church family isn't of our own making but is generated by Him.

As Megan Hill writes in her book *A Place to Belong*, "We do not have to manufacture in our own hearts the love necessary to love a profoundly ordinary—and sometimes difficult—group of people whom we did not choose for ourselves. Instead, the God who loved each one of his people puts his love for them in us."[1]

Thank goodness! I've been acquainted with some of the most fascinating people in my life through the Church. I've sat next to homeless friends, missionaries, mathematicians, and those coming out of twelve-step programs. I've been cornered into extended conversations with close talkers more times than I would like, and sometimes it's been hard to make an exit. The truth is that although it doesn't always feel beautiful, it's ever holy. All these people are God's people—members of *His* family, members of *our* Christian family.

Difficult people can push our buttons, but we must consider God's greater purpose in placing us next to one another. I have a friend who has a hard time interacting with her husband's family. Her mother-in-law hovers, pressuring my friend to an unrealistic standard of motherhood. Despite the strain, my friend has learned to verbalize her boundaries and appreciate her mother-in-law for loving her husband and children. She is part of the meaningful fabric of their lives. We make space for the difficult and help bear the burdens of those we love.

Merging your life with someone else's can be difficult. Whether it's in the context of a marriage, a friendship, a workplace, or the Church, there may be unsolicited advice, off-color remarks, substance abuse, and just plain old baggage that makes relationships difficult. Yet you know those closest to you better when you know their quirky family members or the secrets they've struggled to overcome. In the same way, it's simply not possible to grasp the depth of God's Spirit without presence.

Being Present Now

My sister's church makes T-shirts that read, "No perfect people allowed." And boy, don't people in the Church live up to that? I have cringed many times in the past several years watching brothers and sisters in Christ do damage in His name. *But we are not really that powerful.* God is so in love with His people that He had this to say about anyone or anything that would attempt to bring the Church down:

> "I tell you, you are Peter, and on this rock I will
> build my church, and the gates of hell shall not
> prevail against it."
> MATTHEW 16:18, ESV

Christianity isn't going anywhere. The Church will be around for eternity. Jesus' name will not be trampled. He's beckoning you to "taste and see" the goodness of life in Him (Psalm 34:8).

Before we get frazzled about action steps, let's turn to Scripture. Jesus said, "Come to me, all you who are weary and burdened, and I will give you rest" (Matthew 11:28). It's in the presence of community that we often find this rest for our souls. For example, how many times over the years have I admitted to my church friends that I wasn't feeling close to God? And in how many of those times did it help *just to say it out loud to people who cared*? Every time. Releasing the thing in honesty to a group of fellow believers can often provide the rest you need to keep going.

In his book *A Time to Heal*, J. R. Briggs writes about "ordinary opportunities" in faith community that possess the power for healing and growth to occur in people's lives: "All that it requires is to just show up. . . . There is power in presence."[2]

Presence, community, and speaking our desires out loud—along with the doubt and confusion they may bear—are part of the process. Showing up is an action. Speaking is an action. Such actions create positive momentum and possess eternal value.

Digital Is No Substitute

In this smartphone-convenience culture, where human interaction is routinely avoided, acts of charity and hospitality aren't even carried out face to face. Our charitable giving and keyboard activism are chosen, processed, and siloed through online portals. But it's human touch—skin to skin, voice to voice at gathering places—that syncs charity and justice to the Church. Here there is fellowship and ministry that begins to help heal wounds, restore hearts, and infuse Kingdom love into life and liturgy.

"To touch is to be vulnerable," writes Lore Wilbert in *Handle with Care*, "And to be touched is to be vulnerable too."[3] Vulnerability is medicine. Physical touch is healing. Presence brings this to the surface.

Consider a time when presence has mattered deeply for you. To be physically surrounded and supported by other humans can be the most vitalizing experience—think of sports victories and graduation celebrations, birthday parties and wedding receptions. These are often some of our favorite memories precisely because of the people who are part of them.

I'll never forget when my college basketball team reached the final four in the national championship. This is Indiana, the land of *Hoosiers* (the classic high school basketball movie starring Gene Hackman), a place where most driveways feature worn hoops and small towns celebrate high school stars like royalty. The year Indiana University went to the final game of the NCAA was incredible. The student body gathered around television sets in various bars, restaurants, and living rooms, all convening in hope of a victory. English majors bonded with chemistry majors over favorite players and bets over how far we could go. There was joy, camaraderie, inclusion, and hope.

Obviously, a basketball game is not the same as the Spirit-infused gathering of the Church, but this is an example of a time when people gathering in the flesh made a moment better than it ever could have been if experienced alone. It is symbolic of the powerful communal bonds that sustain our lives, the ones we cultivate through intentional faith.

We Can Lighten Up

There are plenty of nonspiritual moments in gathering—those times that are just fun. Just because church can get serious doesn't mean that we have to be all the time. When I was in college, I lived in a beautiful, old house with nine other women. It was a fun environment, but I worked a lot. One day I came home after work and found some of the girls hanging out, laughing hysterically and eating brownies. They told me a funny story about something that had happened that night, and I was immediately sad I'd missed it.

"I wish I had been here," I said as I pouted, to which my friend Sara replied, "You need to just be around. This stuff happens all the time, but it's not planned. You just have to be here."

I've never forgotten that. I was so busy pouring myself into schoolwork and being obsessed with making money as a waitress and ensuring that I didn't miss any fun nights out with my other friends that I was rarely home, where the good, deep, genuine conversations among these women took place. Looking back, I'm still sad that I so often chose going out to bars and working double shifts over cultivating deep roots with women who might have strengthened my faith and given me a more meaningful sense of place and community during that time in life. Of the eleven women who lived there while I did, I only remain friends with one. I remember them all fondly, but our relationships never deepened because of my lack of presence.

At this point, none of us are probably weighing the bars versus a night on the couch. We are busy women and moms, deep in the trenches of life. But we still have to *be* there—in the building or in the living room or at the dinner—for the magical community moments that just happen. They can't be planned—they are just moments that occur when we consistently show up. Presence cultivates seeds of relationship, and in the right seasons, they blossom. For those with high-risk health concerns, presence may not be as simple as showing up. But I would still encourage as much interaction as possible, whether through screens, on phone calls, or in socially distanced outdoor spaces.

You might accomplish your to-do list every week, but are you building the life you want? Your hunger for deeper spiritual meaning and a closer relationship with God will not happen without putting effort in. "Nobody gains a heavenly mindset passively," my pastor said one Sunday. "You seek after it, you pursue it, because it's not osmosis."

It's time to act. Are you ready?

CHAPTER 17

Our Kids

WHY CHURCH MATTERS FOR THEM

When my first child was born, I intended to breastfeed him. In fact, when the nurse asked me, "Breast or bottle feeding?" I thought it was a weird question. Outside of a medical problem, why would anyone choose not to breastfeed? I had read *What to Expect When You're Expecting* and a stack of other recommended titles, but nothing prepared me for the knifing pain of latching. I thought I'd get used to it, feed the baby when he was hungry, and get on with my day. Instead, I spent the first month of my son's life wedged into a rocking chair desperately coaxing nourishment into his body.

Every outing was against the clock: *Be back in time to feed the baby. Feed the baby just before leaving so I'll have two hours before my body is needed again.* My baby wouldn't latch correctly, and every new effort seemed to fail. I could never tell if he was getting enough milk, and sometimes he'd be eating for what seemed like hours. The pain never subsided. Sleep never came. Soon he was losing weight, clearly not getting enough nutrition. By the time he was eight weeks old—and I was desperate—I had swapped to full-time formula. The decision was anguishing, compelling many tears (from me!), hours of Google searches, and phone calls in an attempt to gain assurance that I wouldn't mortally wound him with formula.

To put it mildly, parenthood transformed my personal paradigm. Immediately, this smooth-skinned little spit-up monster's needs came before mine. Postpartum life created an otherworldly anxiety I'd never known. I drove the car at twenty miles an hour, watched his rising chest when a questionable cough arose. After giving him a clean bill of health and waiting for me to clear the subsequent tears from my eyes, the pediatrician we'd seen multiple unnecessary times gently suggested that I make an appointment with a psychologist for extreme anxiety. Having children changes everything.

Maybe you've been there—with the breastfeeding or just the anxiety or depression. Parenting can be terrifying, and it autopopulates your life priorities anew in every season.

As Christians, we also pray that our babies will know God, that they will inherit our faith and choose to incorporate it into their lives someday. These days, my daily prayers for my kids include that they will love Jesus and be led in the way of

His life. We all want the best things about ourselves to show up in our kids and the worst things to quietly melt away.

I understood God in a new dimension after becoming a parent, finally comprehending the tender way He loves me unconditionally. I also realized quickly how little control I have over my children, including in matters of faith. But I know that I want to deliver the best opportunity for them to choose Jesus. I can do that, and it starts now.

The Most Important People in the Building

My old pastor liked to remind our congregation that the most important people in our church aren't listening to the sermon but are upstairs in their classrooms. Children at church are not an afterthought.

Children's ministry leaders know that decisions for Christ are most often made in childhood, inside the church building. This is why the planning and purpose behind kids' ministry decisions are priorities for churches everywhere and why parents carefully weighed how they could safely return or soundly provide church-based learning from a distance after the pandemic hit. Ultimately, the weight of salvation may rest with these choices.

Think about this: About 78 percent of agnostics are not parents.[1] Faith is often revived or rediscovered in new-parenthood. A friend of mine who grew up with little religious background—and whom I'd never known to attend church—surprised me when a few months after her daughter was born she prayed before we ate lunch together. "Since when do you pray before meals?" I asked her. She replied that she'd recently become a praying woman, specifically because she had become a mom.

If there's even a chance that we can affect our children's lives and eternal futures in some significant way by introducing a strong faith to them, it's worth every bit of discomfort, doubt, and disruption of routine.

Along with the grace we've received in Jesus Christ, our children are some of the gifts we most don't deserve. If passing on the Christian faith to your kids is important to you, you have an incredible opportunity. You will have a dramatic impact on the rest of their lives by how you guide them in faith-related matters now. The choice about how to proceed with children's faith care is far from inconsequential. One survey found that at least two-thirds of Christians become believers before the age of eighteen, and another survey found that 43 percent of Christians come to Christ before the age of twelve.[2] Barna Group found that after parents, guidance for spiritual formation falls on the Church.[3] Childhood is a critical time for shaping faith for a lifetime, and most people need that foundation if they are to practice faith when they are older.

Just as you carefully consider childcare, education, nutrition, and personal development, faith care for our children is no small decision. Leaving church is a great risk for more reasons than one.

A firm faith foundation contributes to a happier, more grounded life. Some parents are worried about feeding faith to their children before they can make a real choice, but studies show providing a faith foundation is better than hoping out kids will make the right decision later on in life.

Psychologist Erica Komisar wrote in the *The Wall Street Journal* that she counsels nonreligious parents to "lie" to their children, telling them that God does exist, simply because of the massive benefits of belief to their long-term mental health.[4] Even on a secular level, this stuff matters.

And then there's this: Children who believe in God are also far less anxious and more hopeful for the course of their lives. Both a 2018 study in the *American Journal of Epidemiology* and a Harvard study of religious involvement among children found that children who attended a religious service at least once per week scored higher on psychological well-being measurements and had lower risks of mental illness.[5] Talk about making a difference in the lives of children!

Brittany's Story

Brittany McKenzie is a Christian mom of four young boys. Growing up, her parents didn't take her to church, but she had two friends in middle school who invited her regularly. Her parents had no problem with her attending, and it was there, inside the church walls, that she developed a relationship with Christ. Though she strayed from her faith during college, God found her again when she decided to attend church while visiting home on winter break.

A video testimony played a divine role in transforming

her life in adulthood, but looking back, she credits her child-hood experiences with building the foundation that enabled her to grow substantially later.

"The seeds planted during my childhood from friends willing to take me to church gave me a place where I felt welcome," she said in an email. One of those friends gave her a Bible as well. Those invitations and that Bible were what God used to change Brittany's life forever.

"I remember opening it to the book of James and under-standing the Scriptures for the first time," she said, remem-bering how her Christian friends' faithful pursuit of her changed her life.

It's wonderful that Brittany had friends who followed God's lead to invite her to church, but as Christian parents, we don't have to rely on the evangelism of others. In fact, our kids could become the ones who invite friends like Brittany themselves! We have the opportunity to be a bridge to the Lord for our kids. We have the power to set them on the divine path with the intentional choices we make today.

Meanwhile, changes in our church-attendance patterns can deeply affect our kids.

When Breanne, whom I wrote about earlier, stopped taking her children to church, she began to notice subtle negative changes in them. It caused her to question whether keeping the kids out of church was really the best idea. "I definitely saw the difference in their lives between the times they were going to church and the times they weren't," she said. "Even at their little ages, it made a difference."

She said that their attitudes shifted, they became more critical, and they lost their felt connection to God when the family stopped praying together. Breanne says that there's no way around the fact that her spiritual crisis was reverberating back onto her children. "If I'm struggling, then they're struggling," she said. She wants her kids to have a faith foundation and knows that staying away from church is destructive in that sense.

During the height of the pandemic, our church was closed. At the time, I lamented the fact that my kids weren't being taught about God in any structured setting. Sure, I implemented prayer and attempted to read through daily toddler Bible stories with my two-year-old and four-year-old, but my efforts were often torpedoed by arguments or wandering eyes. I still believe that my efforts were and are worthwhile, but I felt like the kids were missing out on the benefits that I'd received as a young child in Sunday school. The pandemic isn't the only reason church has been off the table for families though. Sometimes it's a job-related scenario for those who work weekends or a family one for those who care for an elderly parent or a special-needs child. There are seasons for this, but there are also things we can do to keep ourselves and our families on track.

During one season of my life, work was starting to pick up, and I needed childcare. When a local church preschool and day care came highly recommended, I knew that it was the right path because of how important it was to me that they be in a learning environment where faith was a priority.

Non-faith-based day care is a fine alternative, but there are choices we can make to incorporate more faith-based instruction into our kids' lives, and I thought this could be one of them.

When I walked in and saw Bible verses on the walls and coloring sheets with Jesus on them and heard the teachers educating my kids in faith, I knew I had made the right decision.

Spiritual Homeschool

The reality is that as parents we are instilling a worldview in our children. It's just a matter of deciding which worldview we think is most valuable. Our kids are our most important disciples—the gift and responsibility God has given us to lead faithfully.

One of the most beautiful things about the Christian faith is that we are given the freedom to choose to accept the gift of salvation or not—and that is something we can convey to our children from day one. We cannot control the forces of the world, but we can guide our children as we pursue our own trust-based relationship with God on the matter. One example of how we can parent through doubt stands out to me.

Josh McDowell is one of the most respected Christian authors of our time. He raised his children in church, but when his son, Sean, was in his late teens, Sean began to doubt. He discovered ample public pushback to his father's book, a popular publication about the truth of Jesus called

Evidence That Demands a Verdict. The criticism he found online rocked his faith.

On *The Alisa Childers Podcast*, Sean recalled his time of doubt. "*Oh my goodness,*" he'd wondered. "*My parents mean well, but what if I'm wrong? . . . If this isn't true, this changes everything.*"[6]

Rather than reject faith entirely, he started digging, even bringing his honest concerns to his dad, who provided a beautiful example of how we can respond to our kids should something like this happen.

Josh told Sean that his searching was good news, which isn't what you might have expected. The elder McDowell assured his son that the goal was to "seek after truth," not be indoctrinated with religion.[7]

Given the freedom to pursue his questions, Sean was able to rely on his foundation of faith to guide him toward the truth. Over time, he reaffirmed his Christian faith and is now passionate about leading young Christians through their doubts and questions. It's the foundation he had built over time that allowed him the space and strength to question and to discover the truth safely.

Remove the religion and the rules, and lay your children's faith lives before the Lord. If you are pursuing Him yourself, that will naturally affect them.

When we break down the most important things in life, don't our children always top the list? Their potential; their faith; their growth, health, and opportunities. It is worth it for us to break through the protective shell we've built to offer them a faith tinged not with grief but with hope.

Maya Angelou is often quoted as saying, "When you know better, you do better." We are learning that the church of our past is not the church of our future, that we mustn't blindly accept things we've learned, that we can create a new way to embrace faith—one that leads to a life of flourishing in grace, peace, and hope.

Christine Caine has said, "God never consults your past to make your future."[8] Let's not live as if He does.

It's Not All on You

The pressure is not all on you. It never is. It doesn't matter how many parenting books you read or podcasts you listen to, every child is their own beautiful battle, and part of being a Christian parent is entrusting your children to God.

We know that Jesus has a special place in His heart for kids. Most famously, He said to "let the little children come to me, and do not hinder them, for the kingdom of heaven belongs to such as these" (Matthew 19:14). The Kingdom *belongs* to them—it's theirs first before it is anyone else's. They are born with an intrinsic kinship with God. How we lead them in childhood can help keep that familial bond in place or make it loosen as they grow.

It's not on you to save your children, but Jesus does encourage us not to hinder them. Opening the pathway to faith by attending church, praying together, reading Scripture, and worshiping God in the home are ways to help ensure that you don't hinder them in any way. He has entrusted us with these children, whom He calls a gift (Psalm 127:3, NLT), to guide them toward His truth and mercy. And the good news is that He will be with you all the way in it. In Isaiah, it is written that God "gently leads those that have young" (Isaiah 40:11).

As a kid, I sang a song that put it simply: "Look up when the going's really tough. Look up—God is more than big enough!" Silly kids' songs are sometimes the very best reminders of the truth about God. What we learn in childhood is sealed in our minds for a lifetime, and that matters.

Years ago, I heard about a woman who was grocery shopping, reeling with depression about some difficult life circumstances. Making her way through the produce aisle, a toddler burst out in a classic song from the cartoon *Veggie Tales*, singing, "God is bigger than the boogie man!"[9] In that moment, God spoke to her through the song, reminding her that He *is* bigger than the problems that were plaguing her. The fact that many of us can so clearly recall some of the words from songs about God that we learned as children exemplifies the sustainability of faith seeds. God Himself is waiting to guide you in planting these seeds. I say this not to shame you for what you haven't done as a parent yet but to empower you in your next parenting step. In Christ, we have freedom from the past and hope for the future.

CHAPTER 18

Our Belonging

"Just do it" is probably the most genius slogan ever invented. It can cover nearly any challenge, discomfort, or fear—and Nike has certainly used the phrase to the max. I've used it to force myself into things I didn't really feel like doing several times, including when I was seeking Christian community as a young adult. At the time, I was haphazardly attending a church, but didn't know anyone well. I signed up for a small group in the hope that it would lead to friendships, or at least something to help quell my growing depression.

As I drove into a retirement community and found a parking spot the first night, I wondered if I had the wrong address. An elderly woman answered the door, opening it to reveal a home dusted with pink antique china, comfy quilted afghans, and monochrome photos mounted in fancy gold frames.

Dorothy, I soon discovered, was ninety years old, though she moved as if she were thirty years younger. Her soft, dewy skin and sharp mind made it hard to believe she'd been born close to the turn of the twentieth century.

As young women trickled in for the group meeting, I think we were all a little surprised at being placed in a group with a woman born seven decades before us. But now I see what an incredible opportunity it was. That first night, Dorothy told us about her daily ritual of waking up every day and, before touching her feet to the ground, saying, *Good morning, Father. Good morning, Jesus. Good morning, Holy Spirit*—an intentional practice she'd begun years ago.

This meeting set the stage for the next year, during which we would dive into Scripture and the struggles of twenty-year-old girls putting together their adult lives for the first time. Some of the girls had heavy grief (two had recently lost a sister, another a parent), and others were dealing with health issues.

As we discussed college courses, first jobs, budding relationships, doubts, and spiritual struggles, Dorothy could address them with the loving discernment of a decades-long follower of Christ, someone who had been married and widowed, seen war and peace, and lived through the Great Depression and at least twelve American presidents.

We may have been privileged college girls, but our struggles were real. Learning to be vulnerable at a young age and taking our anguish to God in the company of others were important actions and part of building lasting faith. Being part of this church group became an anchor for my life at the time. It is obvious that God led me to this particular group, where I could watch a woman who was still choosing Him faithfully at ninety years old. It was something I could never have encountered had I not been committed to that urge to "just do it"—a nudge from God to join with these particular saints here on earth in the beautiful community He provided for me.

Even in her old age—when so many become complacent or too weak to make an effort—Dorothy valued and understood the importance of church community and building the next generation of believers. When young and old commune together, we see a very cool example of intergenerational unity in Christ.

You aren't likely to meet someone like Dorothy if you stay within the confines of where you are now. It's one more thing I love about the Church: We are smashed together with people very different from ourselves whose faith lives and experiences are uniquely seasoned. Imagine adding the rich flavor of Dorothy's life experience to your faith journey. Imagine forging a relationship with someone who grew up very differently than you did and learning from their distinctive insights, ones that you'll miss if you stay within the confines of your own comfort zone.

Today, the girls from that group are stay-at-home moms, artists, scientists, ministry leaders, and more. Dorothy has long since passed away, but her legacy of faithfulness lives on in the many women she mentored and invested in as one who was steadfast in God's call on her life.

What might you be missing by staying in a comfort zone of online church or a bubble of busyness?

In addition to Dorothy, there have been others I'd likely not have gotten to know if I weren't in church community with them. Sarah has had a tough life. She grew up in various foster homes and has been fending for herself for years. She's fifteen years younger than me, has two little girls, and currently works nights at a gas station to pay the bills.

When we struck up a conversation after church one day, I felt God urging me to invite her over and be a resource in whatever way I could. Since her girls are younger than my daughter, I now bag up all my daughter's clothes and get them ready for Sarah to take. I check in with her from time to time and regularly pray for her family. Her job has made it impossible for her to attend church recently, but I consider her part of my church family in Christ.

I know and believe relationships like this make a difference. Sarah knows she's loved and supported at our church—and that we will be there for her when she needs us. I watched her baptism two years ago, and seeing this strong, courageous girl go under the water and emerge renewed in her relationship with Christ was a moment I'll never forget. Seeing someone's life changed by the gospel will never get old. And that tends to happen often when we are engaged in the community where it is ripe to happen.

If anyone is in Christ, he is a new creation; old things have passed away; behold, all things have become new.

2 CORINTHIANS 5:17, NKJV

In Christ, we are not separated by our color or class, sexuality or ethnicity. Our alikeness, our newness, is found in our allegiance to God, who unifies us in the pages of Scripture and the Spirit of His love in our hearts. At the same time, we can celebrate and appreciate our unique differences in appearance, culture, and life experience. Such things are not barriers to being known but vibrant additions to our lives together. The world will tell us we are separated by such details, but we know that these differences make us a better Church together in the world.

As Christians, we have a stronger bond with fellow believers than we could with anyone else. Our eternal identity in Christ binds us together to overcome any other label that may identify us here on earth. "There is neither Jew nor Gentile, neither slave nor free, nor is there male and female, for you are all one in Christ Jesus," says the apostle Paul in Galatians 3:28.

To this I say, "Amen!"

Dinner with Sinners

Even with what we've just covered, I know fears or anxieties about church and church community may remain. In the past, I've heard people say that church isn't for "people like me." This makes me want to wrap my arms around them and say, "That's not true—it's for people *just like* you!"

In the Gospel of Mark, we read that Jesus dined with "many tax collectors and other disreputable sinners" and that "there were many people of this kind among Jesus' followers." When Jesus was scolded by the Pharisees for hanging out with these kinds of people, He said these famous words: "Healthy people don't need a doctor—sick people do. I have come to call not those who think they are righteous, but those who know they are sinners" (Mark 2:15-17, NLT).

It reminds me of a recent TikTok video I saw. The voice-over words say this: "I'm here to tell you right now: We don't care. [Laughter.] We don't care!"[1] And that's what I want to say to you: Jesus doesn't care! We don't care! We want *you*—literally the way you are today, right now, baggage and sin and anger and doubt and all the things. Just come on in to dinner with the rest of us sinners and tax collectors.

Those who have questions no one has wanted to answer in the past—get in here. Those worn out by motherhood and busy schedules—welcome! I am confident in speaking for God's Church: *We want you here.* If the life clutter of the past and present has buried your invitation to God's house beneath fear, busyness, discomfort, or the tyranny of indecision, let's dig it out. You are *so* invited.

I don't usually recommend having FOMO (fear of missing out), but in this case I do. You *should* fear missing out on what God has for you! Fear missing the transformation, healing, and growth that will happen when you invest in your faith life through church community. The incredible work He does through His Church didn't stop in 2020 just because the world did. Many of us have noticed that God seems to be doing some incredible things in the hearts of Christians around the world right now. For example, the global Church is thriving even in the face of deep persecution. God often shows up powerfully as we face tragedy, troubles, and trials. Don't miss His message.

Be Where You Are

I'll never forget attending a church event where the speaker shared her story of actively walking through a divorce. It wasn't down the road, after she'd processed and learned—it was happening currently. Her speech that day was one that some might have been ashamed or embarrassed to share, but she blessed me deeply because of her willingness to share her grief with us. She didn't know what the rest of us were going through, but I can imagine others had been where she was, divorced or hurt or angry. It taught me that I shouldn't be scared to openly share my struggles, that church community is a safe place to grieve and grow.

Her ability to speak God's truth and connect with our group in the middle of her pain said more to me than any put-together woman with a neatly packaged personal story ever could have. It inspired me to never wait—to always be willing to share, even in the middle of my mess. God is faithful then, too, and I don't want anyone to forget that.

Resisting Faith Comparison

Despite knowing that we are welcome in our mess, I've often envied Christians whose kindness and generosity seem ripped from the lines of 1 Corinthians 13. Like they believe they might "[entertain] angels unawares" (Hebrews 13:2, ESV)—and actually live like it! I've heard myself say, "Oh, she's so good" or "I love her; she's so sweet" while wishing I were more like her. Is there anyone in your life you would never dare say a curse word around? Or someone you are on your best behavior with because they seem so pious?

I'll never forget traveling by cab with Jennifer,[2] a woman I consider a mentor in the faith and one of the most prayer-centered people I've ever met. She went out of her way to be sure our Uber driver felt cared for and loved, asking him questions about his life and home and leaving him an extra-big tip. "I just want to make sure he felt loved today," she told me as we walked into our meeting.

This is just one example of the many ways I have seen her take the call to love others—the stranger—as if they were Jesus Himself. If you reveal to her an issue you're struggling with, she will listen closely and immediately grab your hand and say a prayer out loud for you. She is unashamed of her faith in God to accomplish His will and come to our rescue. I've often felt inadequate next to her example. *Palms up, Lord*, she often says, physically lifting her palms to the heavens. It means *Whatever You have for me, God, I'm here for it.*

It can be easy to compare yourself to someone like her and feel like any effort you put forward will never be good enough. Let's be honest: It won't be! It isn't for Jennifer, for me, or for you.

But if we cower in the shadow of a perceived "greater" faith, we may never live out the one God has given us specifically. Jennifer is as extroverted and charismatic as they come, a born leader. We are not all created to be this way, and we must embrace our God-given strengths and weaknesses. As it's often said, comparison is the thief of joy. You may not be whatever Christian comes to mind for you as you read this. But none of us are "good enough" without the saving grace of Jesus Christ. The playing field is dead even.

Even Your Worst Isn't Bad Enough

It's scary to admit this to you here, but I genuinely want you to know that even those who appear good on the outside have ugly demons in their pasts. Memories of past drinking and youthful drifting from my faith have caused me great anguish. These recollections are studded with the shame and guilt of decisions made on late evenings or other destructive moments in time when I tried to vanquish my fears of insufficiency with alcohol or personal recklessness.

I still have guttural flashbacks and struggle to reconcile who I am with the girl I was then. For a long time, these things made me feel like I wasn't like other people at church. Those couple of years were some of the only times in my life that I haven't regularly shown up at church. It turns out it's tough to keep living in sin when you're confronted with truth in the pew.

I often heard a voice in my head asking, *What kind of Christian engages in that kind of behavior?* We all have the capacity to do really bad things, but it doesn't mean we aren't welcome to come before God.

But what I know is this: I'm forgiven. What I know is this: God wouldn't want me to feel excluded from His holy community because of something I did years ago. Even if it was yesterday, He wouldn't want that for me. Nor does He want it for you. Every one of us is an image bearer, fully restored by the riches of His grace the moment we accept Jesus. It's hard to believe, but that is the passion of our God.

Assumptions about what others might think of us are often elaborate creations of our own making. And we forget that the other people in the pews (or on the couches or seated at coffee tables next to us) have their own difficult pasts.

Hypocrites?

When my husband first started attending church with me, he was always on the defense. He thought all Christians were hypocrites (which, honestly, we all are in some way or another!) and was self-conscious about his tattooed arms and abuse-filled past.

Within months of starting to attend church together, we heard from a pastor who had battled depression his entire life and attempted suicide. Another time, we heard from someone who had been born to a single mother at a time when that just wasn't a thing. Their stories helped us feel embraced by the church, as if it would be okay for them to know our stories too.

I've spoken with women at my church who have had abortions they regret, people who are struggling to stay sober even as they show up each week, and those with doubts a mile long. But you know what? I'm glad they come anyway. I'm glad they face the discomfort that weighs against them to show up and be in the presence of God. There is no better place to be.

These days, my husband no longer flings around the word *hypocrite* so freely, and you'll often find him setting up chairs for the service or teaching middle schoolers in Sunday school. He grew up in an abusive, traumatic household and experimented with many drugs as a young man. He's also been divorced and diagnosed with bipolar disorder and PTSD, yet you would never know these things when he welcomes you to our church on Sunday morning.

His example is far from isolated. Four in ten women who have had an abortion say that they are churchgoers.[3] Countless people in our congregations are addicted to alcohol and living as if they aren't. Church people may not appear to be like you on the surface, but we are all linked by our fallen humanity. In Christ, our identity is one: We are all saints in the everlasting Kingdom.

In 1 Corinthians, Paul explicitly calls God's people saints:

> To the church of God that is in Corinth, to those
> sanctified in Christ Jesus, called to be saints together
> with all those who in every place call upon the name
> of our Lord Jesus Christ, both their Lord and ours . . .
>
> I CORINTHIANS I:2, ESV

We may refer to particularly good or pious people as saints in jest, but the truth is that as Christians we are all saints because of our place in the family of God. This title is a clear representation of the fact that our sins have been erased by grace. In what other realm could someone like me or you be called an actual saint? Only in the upside-down Kingdom of Jesus. And only in the community of believers called the Church will this name begin to feel fitting.

As Megan Hill writes in *A Place to Belong*, "In the church, we all have one testimony. We are the people God has called."[4]

Your fellow churchgoers are brothers and sisters, saints like yourself—fallen but forgiven. Ephesians 2:12-13 (ESV) lays it out plainly for us:

> Remember that you were at that time separated from Christ [that's all of us!] . . . having no hope and without God in the world. But now in Christ Jesus you who once were far off have been brought near by the blood of Christ [again, that's all Christians!].

A few verses later, Paul writes that we are "no longer strangers and aliens" but "fellow citizens with the saints and members of the household of God" (Ephesians 2:19, ESV).

You are welcome, you are loved, and you are accepted.

PART THREE

A Call Worth Pursuing

CHAPTER 19

Our Authenticity

BEING WHO WE ARE

Rich Mullins was an extremely successful Christian record-ing artist, crafting songs with lyrics about the simple things of life: taking one step at a time, Christmas morning, the color green. He visited my church in the early 1990s for a concert, and I saw him—long hair like Jesus would have had (at least that's how my nine-year-old self translated it)—walking barefoot down the thin-blue-carpeted hallway beneath shocking bright lights. As I watched him chat with people, it pricked the confines of my mind that he would be comfortable enough to just kick off his shoes like that. This was God's house, and the people inside were his family members. He was welcome to make himself at home—and he *totally* knew it.

That's an assumption we all make when gathering with other believers. We *can* be presumptive about our belonging in the communion of saints because we're told we belong by God Himself. The space doesn't belong to the pastor—it belongs to God. Sometimes I think we elevate church buildings, thinking of them as places that are so holy we can't get comfortable. We chide our children to be on their best behavior, worried that the imperfections of life at home may seep out. We turn the car around when fighting ensues or tears erupt. I get it, but I don't want the realities of life to be barriers to God's best for you.

The other week, I was arguing with my husband and had one kid unhappy with her dirty shoes and another refusing to eat breakfast, and we barely got out the door. We walked into church disheveled and stressed, ready to drop the kids off at Sunday school and not feeling much like worshiping.

As the music started, I just felt off and wandered into the hallway to find two friends chatting. I walked up, and they asked how I was doing. Within seconds, I unloaded the rough morning and the stressful past week—the first of my oldest going to kindergarten and loaded with unexpected struggles.

Unpacking what was on my mind as the three of us talked it through was a relief. "I'm surprised we're even here this morning," I admitted. And as I said it, I realized how glad I was that we were, that I was able to share this real-life moment with them. Within a few moments, I was ready to head back into the service and sing a couple of songs before the sermon. I was brighter, lighter, and feeling closer to God after having received the blessing of my friends in the hallway. This wouldn't have happened had I not persisted in getting myself to church that day.

Just as You Are

You can be a Christian in the local church just as you are—in the middle of all your mess. It's the very best place to be. I've been that person many times—hungover, bloated, and miserable from a night of bingeing and purging, barreling through the service with a broken heart. Those are the days I've cried through worship, had to slurp back my sobs during the sermon, and not been able to say much to anyone afterward. But I was there. And there are people there with you, sharing the same kinds of doubts, pains, traumas, and fears you may be holding. Speak it out loud, and you will be shocked at the "Me toos" that appear.

Inside or outside the church, we have only broken people to lean on. But inside, gathering with the power of the Holy Spirit as our guide, we can begin to heal from the inside out.

It can be long and hard and ugly. But it's necessary if we are to ever cross the threshold to a more authentic and personal faith. You've probably heard it before, this concept that you can't go around your problems; rather, you have to go through them. The spiritual desires we have are not quenched by anything other than the one true God—and He does this through the sacred tool of His Kingdom, the Church.

What the Old Testament Taught Me

I felt like I got to know God so much better by reading through the entire Old Testament last year. Even though parts of it were tough, I saw parts of God that were new to me, ways that He works I'd not seen before. In the past, I'd always been taught to focus on some key figures—Abraham, Moses, Noah. What struck me during this reading was this: The real starring role of the Old Testament (apart from God Himself) goes to the Israelites—God's people. While as individuals they certainly had their own personal relationships with God, God clearly expressed a collective love for them as a people. He brought *them* out of Egypt. He led *them* through the desert. He brought *them* to the Promised Land. It wasn't about one family, or one person, but a Kingdom of people—what you might call the Church.

The Kingdom is still alive today. God is guiding us as one body to something great, something that will ultimately be fulfilled in heaven but has begun in our lives here on earth. To separate ourselves from the Kingdom is to miss what God is doing through His people—turning the arc of history toward His glory. As we're reminded in His Word,

Do not put your trust in princes,
　　in human beings, who cannot save.
When their spirit departs, they return to the ground;
　　on that very day their plans come to nothing. . . .
He is the Maker of heaven and earth,

the sea, and everything in them—
he remains faithful forever.

PSALM 146:3-4, 6

Do you trust in the Lord? God says that His Church is of utmost importance. He knows how messed up we are, and He definitely knows the faults of the people He's asking you to commune with. But He never stops redeeming us—and He loves every one of them as much as He loves you. He's seen it all—His people have *done* it all. Can you trust in God's declaration that His Church is where you'll find Him?

"I have not come to call the righteous, but sinners," said Jesus in Mark 2:17. His Church is for those experiencing hurt, doubt, stress, trauma, depression, and hunger. Are you ready to have those things healed?

CHAPTER 20

Our Community

FINDING THE RIGHT SPACE AND PLACE

I was recently reading the Gospel of John and noticed something I hadn't before: Jesus says that He is praying not for the world but for you and me (John 17:9). The world is not going to get much better here on earth. Jesus says so plainly; He doesn't even pray for that to happen. But He does pray for *you*, the individual, and for *us*, His Church.

"I am praying not only for these disciples," Jesus said in John 17:20 (NLT), in the days before His death, "but also for all who will ever believe in me through their message." Reading this made me feel a visceral connection to the Jesus who walked the earth, like He was thinking of me in His mind's eye when He said these words. Another thing

John tells us is this: Jesus has revealed God to us—as in, us Christians—and we "do not belong to the world" (John 15:19).

We are His beloved and greatest creation, and He has instilled in us the free will to choose to love Him or not. If you are reading these words, you've probably chosen to love Him. And every other Jesus follower is a fellow sojourner through this world to which we do not belong (and boy, do we feel that on a regular basis!). I felt this recently when I was stumped about what to say in my Instagram bio. Such a little space, but one I wanted to hold great meaning. What did I want people to know about me when they happened upon my tiny squares of life? I settled on this: "Made for another world." It just felt right. It was taken from a C. S. Lewis quote:

> If I find in myself a desire which no experience in this world can satisfy, the most probable explanation is that I was made for another world.[1]

God has a specific purpose for our lives here, and it's fulfilled in part through our Church family. Without the Church, we hand-deliver Satan a foothold in our lives.

"The enemy, content when Christians stay frozen in stagnation, will do everything he can not to wake the believers, lest they again realize their true purpose," writes Mark Sayers.[2]

Our true purpose! What is that? Give it some real thought. Don't just graze over a few Bible verses and offer up a quick prayer before bed. Ponder it with the weight it deserves. Alexandra Hoover, an author and Bible teacher, messages our purpose this way: "Eyes up."[3]

When you are considering the Church, the point of faith in your life, are your eyes inward, outward, or upward? If they aren't on God, you won't get very far, but if you are truly seeking His guidance, He will not leave you hanging.

Neglecting this is the reason there are churches bearing little to no fruit. It's why they are dying. They are unhelpful branches being shorn so that healthy branches can emerge and reinvigorate the cause of Christ. Now is the time to be part of that transformation. Seek out the healthy branches and attach yourself to one.

Finding a Church That Just Might Work

Reaching the conclusion that you want to get back to church and truly invest in your faith is one thing; finding the right place and space to do it is another.

My family and I moved back home to Indiana from a big city where I'd attended a large church that was popular in the area. After settling into a suburb, we were immediately in search of a church to call home. I wasn't sure where to begin—churches dot every corner of the Midwest. I started by Googling "churches near me," but it was clear that many of them weren't showing up. Word of mouth is really the best gauge for authentic responses, so I dove into some local Facebook groups for advice.

I'd loved my previous church, so it was hard to believe we

could find one that checked all the boxes that that one had. I created a list of all the churches that seemed promising, and we began visiting them one by one, baby in tow, not knowing a soul.

After several weeks of church hopping, we found a large church that seemed good enough. It had an atmosphere similar to that of other churches we'd been in, so we attended it for a few months. But something felt off. I wanted a church that was more intimate, a place where the pastor knew who we were.

The first day we attended Waterline Church, we were immediately greeted with handshakes, asked our names, and guided through the process of registering our son for the nursery. Not a moment went by that someone wasn't ushering us somewhere or asking us about ourselves. It felt different from some of the churches we'd sampled, and I was very thankful I hadn't given up searching for the church God had for us.

Six years later, we're still there—as volunteers, attenders, and that family whose kids are known for their crazy antics during the services when there is no children's class. Just last week, my pastor pointed out our kids specifically as staple features of our weekly service. It was both humbling and an honor to know just how much a part of the family we've become.

When you're in a safe community, it's difficult *not* to share hardships with the listening ears and concerned faces turned your way at prayer time. Yes, it's easy to have a "vulnerability hangover" from time to time, but everyone needs a safe space to share life.

At first, the vulnerability made my husband uncomfortable. He'd only attended church as an adult and didn't have much experience a small church setting like this. At our old church, it had been easy enough to slip in and out of service without speaking to anyone. The intimacy of our new church was stressful for an introvert like him.

Within a couple of weeks of the day we started attending, several folks in the front lobby could call us by name. When he skipped a week or two, more than one person asked where he'd been. It was uncomfortable, causing him to announce, "I don't think I like that church."

I called him out, reminding him that he had always said he wanted to go to a smaller church. Now that we were doing that, it took some getting used to. He did, and he's now a beloved member of the church, recognizable to all for his volunteer work.

Get rid of the old rules and the tired narrative that says that you have to act one way, be a member of a particular party, or subscribe to a certain denominational belief system. You don't have to go back to where you used to be, but that doesn't mean there's nowhere else to go.

Microchurch Revolution

Another place you may find some healthy branches is at a microchurch. I'm surprised by how many people are unaware of a church revolution that is taking place all over the country: Thousands of microchurches are opening up nationwide to offer a new option in rural areas, prisons, coffee shops, living rooms, recovery centers, places of work, and more.

The local church is not relegated to a particular blueprint, and God has given an innovative vision to modern Christians about how best to reach and serve people. For example, you can find many places to attend thanks to Fresh Expressions, an organization that exists to help people open churches based on niche demographics (like hobbies, workplaces, and locations). Here you can be connected to gatherings like "Messy Church" (for families) and "Amore Groups" (for married couples), as well as biker church, cowboy church, church for artists, and church after work. And if what you're looking for doesn't exist, you can create it yourself! Even as the world around us grows increasingly post-Christian, these new iterations of church are thriving. God wants us to show up, and He's making a way for us to want to do that no matter where we are or how we feel.

When you finally realize that your most cherished affinities, places, or people can be part of your church experience, returning to church may be less daunting or overwhelming. It may feel natural, as if your spirituality is saturated through the whole of your life—as if your faith is no longer separate from your feelings or failings. Things settle into place when we allow God to guide us and follow His nudges rather than push them away.

CHAPTER 21

Our Society

HOW GOING TO CHURCH
CHANGES THE WORLD

Going to church isn't just about us and our personal spirituality.

The Church is how God works through His people and provides for the vulnerable. It's how He moves heaven and earth to provide peace and freedom—and diapers, breakfast, and Christmas presents for children in impoverished families.

The Church is where God inspires hearts and minds to go out and do good, where His Spirit starts planting seeds in our minds to remind us of what we are here for: to love Him and others.

When I drifted from church (during that rough time I wrote about earlier), I can't help but think about how my lack of presence affected my community. In addition to not being physically present to serve, the minuscule amount I irregularly gave (fifty dollars here, a hundred dollars there, scattered over weeks or months depending on my mood) dissipated to zero quickly. I knew that tithes and offerings are how the local church survives, especially smaller ones, but I wasn't thinking from that perspective when I decided to stop participating.

Because churches are nonprofit entities that function almost exclusively on donations, I knew this was a bad move on my part. But because I wasn't in church regularly to receive reminders about the worthy causes funded by my church, I missed the needs that required funding to survive. I put my blinders on and skimped when it came to tithing so I could afford other, less important things I wanted. When you aren't in the building, it's all too convenient to blow your budget on Amazon and promise you'll tithe next month.

This isn't, however, a chapter about the ins and outs of tithing. Rather, it's about the way generosity and care for the vulnerable are accomplished through the living body of the Church. The truth is, our country needs the Church, and the more people who participate, the better.

For every multimillionaire TV pastor, there are thousands of pastors living modestly and striving to create churches that matter in their communities. Many pastors these days are bivocational, meaning that they moonlight as pastors in addition to working their day jobs. In general, ministry is not a lucrative profession, and most people aren't in it for money.

Most churches are small, struggling, and reliant on tithes

and offerings to pay small salaries and fund important ministries (like diaper drives, food banks, and partnerships with local organizations that help abused women or homeless youth).

Churches are often central partners in community work to refurbish parts of their cities, help with cleanup efforts, or provide free mentorships or physical resources to families in need. At my home church, we partner with the neighborhood to sponsor a Fourth of July festival, and we do the setup and teardown for free. We get our hands dirty to make our community a place of welcome and delight for those who live here. I attended a fish-fry fundraiser at a Methodist church recently, and the hallways were lined with flyers and sign-up sheets for volunteer nursing-home visits and clothing drives for single moms. The church parking lot was a rocky planet of asphalt in need of repavement, but the outreach ministry was moving full speed ahead. This is one of many thousands of churches across the country injecting light and life into the communities around them.

In his book *Church Forsaken*, Jonathan Brooks describes how his church on the south side of Chicago participates in the "collective flourishing" of the community by believing "that the empowerment of the most marginalized and outcast is at the heart of God."[1] The book also documents how too many churches are interested exclusively in soul saving and neglect the holistic care and concern for people's earthly needs. And it's true—plenty of churches aren't focused on the right things, or enough of them.

Churches are required to make their monetary records public, so if you're interested, it's easy to see where a church's spending goes and decide if you're comfortable with the leadership's choices. There's absolutely no need to attend or tithe to a church that isn't using your money in biblically sound ways. Hold tight to the Bible verses that showcase our purpose:

> Do not oppress the widow, the fatherless, the
> sojourner, or the poor, and let none of you devise
> evil against another in your heart.
>
> ZECHARIAH 7:10, ESV

> Thus says the LORD: Do justice and righteousness,
> and deliver from the hand of the oppressor him who
> has been robbed. And do no wrong or violence to
> the resident alien, the fatherless, and the widow, nor
> shed innocent blood in this place.
>
> JEREMIAH 22:3, ESV

It's vital to remember these passages—not necessarily by chapter and verse, but certainly by sentiment and compassion. These are some of our greatest calls, and they are often fulfilled through the mission of the local church.

The Ripple Effect

You may be thinking, *I don't have to go to church to be a generous person.* That's true, but the data show that going to church makes a big difference. Most tithing comes from those who attend church regularly, and the ripple effect on society is unbelievable.

Data and personal stories reveal that church begins to change people for the better from the inside out even when they don't realize it. It can transform individuals and communities in ways that aren't obvious at first. For example, statistics show that just taking the action to attend Sunday services makes us significantly more generous, kind, and compassionate toward our neighbors. It creates a stronger bond among members of the local community and turns newspaper headlines into human faces and prayer requests into tear-stained cheeks you witness in sacred vulnerability.

Churchgoing families tithe to their home churches, but that's merely the starting point of their generosity. They also give exponentially more to other religious and non-religious causes. A 2017 study from the Lilly Family School of Philanthropy found that 62 percent of faithful religious families donate to charities outside the Church while only 46 percent of secular families do.[2]

In the book *American Grace: How Religion Divides and Unites Us*, Robert Putnam and David Campbell share extensive research on how giving practices, from volunteering to donating money, are affected by a person's faith.

They revealed that 88 percent of people who give to religious causes also give to secular causes, like the American Cancer Society, humanitarian aid missions, or even things like the arts or local education initiatives.[3] Someone who attends church weekly has an 81-percent likelihood of donating to secular causes, while someone who doesn't only has a 60-percent likelihood of donating to any cause at all.[4]

Imagine how donations to both secular and faith-based causes will continue to decline as people leave faith communities en masse. Imagine how the COVID-19 pandemic has affected these things—extraordinarily!

People don't decrease their giving on purpose when they aren't in church. It's not a conscious choice. They are no less compassionate or caring; they are simply less aware of being in the vicinity of need, and they lose the opportunity to easily expend their generosity.

Volunteerism and the "good neighbor" landscape follows the same trend. A Gallup survey found that faithful Americans are far more likely to have volunteered their time and helped a stranger in the past month than the nonreligious.[5] A Pew Research Center study on the civic and community engagement of religious Americans reported higher rates of volunteerism, giving, and civic participation among the faithful.[6]

For those who regularly attend church, personal philanthropy and volunteerism skyrocket and empathy for people who are different increases. If there's anything we need in our families, communities, and society right now, that's what it is. We are called to live, love, and serve here on earth to the best of our abilities, and church plays a part in that.

Personal salvation is of utmost importance, but the Church on earth is not just about going to heaven. It's about loving and serving people, both inside and outside the Church, here and now. The moment we become Christians, we are transformed into eternal saints, our souls set on eternity that very instant.

Do we trust God when He says to "test me in [tithing] . . . and see if I will not throw open the floodgates of heaven and pour out so much blessing that there will not be room enough to store it" (Malachi 3:10)?

Throughout the Bible, there is mention of the riches of God's grace, love, mercy, and forgiveness. His riches extend further than any amount of money. God will do better with our one hundred dollars than we could do with one thousand or one million dollars. He'll do more with 10 percent than we can do with 90 percent. Generosity, of course, comes in a variety of packages. Even if money is tight, there are ways to reach out and extend generosity through small favors, kind words, or the donation of time. Whatever we are giving away in God's name and through the power of His Spirit will be blessed.

Helping the Most Vulnerable

For moms, it's easy to identify with other mothers who are struggling. I've seen the power of mommas coming together online to help a fellow sojourner in need. We all know the toll motherhood can take on even the most well-prepared or experienced parent, but some women also face extreme, nearly impossible situations. We may feel stressed to carve out time to attend church, but some women are barely able to cover childcare or make ends meet by working two jobs. One thing the local church can be deft at is identifying the needs of such women and their families. In my church, we have a prayer group on Facebook, and those with needs can post prayer requests or requests for physical help. Many times I've seen a person humbly request help with childcare or rides and another church member graciously step up to meet that need.

I don't know about you, but even the mention of children in foster care causes my heart to skip a beat. Perhaps you've visited a foster-care or adoption website featuring heart-wrenching photos of children hoping to be adopted or in need of long-term care. Most often, the religiously faithful fulfill that need. Sixty-five percent of foster parents attend church weekly.[7] There is something about proximity to God and His people that pushes us toward greater generosity. Knowing this makes me excited to reinvigorate the Church and remind people why being part of it matters so much.

A foundation of love, generosity, and morality in a person's heart is built in the Church; God set it up this way. The Church should be at the heart of your spiritual life, a foundational piece of how you live and move and breathe as a child of God in this world. This may also be why attending church regularly makes such a significant difference in our mental and emotional lives.

CHAPTER 22

Our Rituals

BUILDING A MEANINGFUL LIFE

Christians participate in liturgy and meaningful ritual whether they realize it or not. Each week, we repeat songs, prayers, and actions—symbols representing the language of faith. By integrating these words and ceremonies into our lives consistently, we gain access to their deeper truths when we need them later. When trouble descends, these liturgies, which are embedded in our lives, sustain us. When, in our humanness, we fail, we can mine these precious resources, carved from the ritual of faith. We can then survive off the God-truths lying dormant within us. Absent this spiritual investment, one may be at a loss faith-wise when hardship strikes.

Perhaps you feel like the motions don't matter. We all

know how it feels to go through them with little enthusiasm. But what if we intentionally put meaning behind them? Whether you know it or not, rituals and habits contextualize meaning in our lives.

I see this in nightly prayers with my son, feel it in the memory of my wedding vows, taste it in the sour grape juice of Communion, hear it in the engine of my dad's revving motorcycle on the way to birthday breakfasts. I remember it when I think of the weekends spent spooning out grapefruits with my grandma on her kitchen floor, in the summers I sipped cherry Slush Puppies on a rocky lakeshore with my mom.

Many of our biggest life moments are based in ritual or liturgy. When a baby arrives, a pink or blue hat is snuggled atop their coned head moments after birth. We wear weird, boxy hats and fist pump our diplomas when we graduate, and we toast with slim, bubbly glasses of champagne on New Year's Eve. We accept engagement with a diamond ring and stand before a sacred, cross-laden altar to marry the one we love. We shave our legs twice a week, wash the sheets once, and always load the dishwasher before bed. It makes us feel good to stick to our rituals. It helps life make sense.

These innocent rituals showcase the power that even unimportant habits in our life have. How much more relevant are the rituals connected to our deeply held faith beliefs? And most of these involve other people—reading the Gospels together on Christmas Eve, saying family prayers before dinner, singing songs about Jesus to our babies in moonlit rockers.

Somewhere in adulthood—in the thick of motherhood,

the pandemic, life—it became easy to let our rituals die. Our communities dissipated into digital gatherings all too easy to opt out of. Before the pandemic, I absolutely loved going to my small group each week. I wrote earlier about how meaningful that group was for me. When we switched to Zoom meetings, I was less compelled to attend. Even when I did, I found myself multitasking or mindlessly glancing at social-media notifications. The women were the same, but the environment stripped away the humanity. As we entered 2021, still meeting on Zoom, I had barely made a meeting in months. I can only imagine where other women fell on the spectrum of being Facebook Live/Zoomed out. There were a million lifelines, but I fell out of the habit of connecting.

It's a common trend that has hurt us all in one way or another. Both connection and ritual are vital to our mental health. As Casper ter Kuile writes in his book *The Power of Ritual*, "In the midst of a crisis of isolation, where loneliness leads to deaths of despair, being truly connected isn't a luxury. It's a lifesaver."[1]

You may not be dying of despair, but are you pining for embodied soul care via community and meaningful ritual? Friendships and community are not a luxury but lifeblood. Biblical community feeds us in a very particular way that cannot happen elsewhere. Tish Harrison Warren gets it in her book *Liturgy of the Ordinary*:

> Christian friendships are call-and-response
> friendships. We tell each other over and over, back

and forth, the truth of who we are and who God is. Over dinner and on walks, dropping off soup when someone is sick, and in prayer over the phone, we speak the good news to each other. And we become good news to every other.[2]

There's a supernatural accountability there, a constant reminder of the goodness of God, a call to love our neighbors well and a built-in prompt to call one another back to our faith in times of struggle. Our habits, our community, our rituals—they guide us toward a larger, better expectation of ourselves.

If you don't step back and evaluate where your life is tracking, you may miss the trajectory you want. A wonderful God and a wholly embodied faith give us signposts for the right road—and Scripture always has the answer for our wandering. Let's think about those meaningful rituals that so deeply root us.

What does it mean that I always say "I love you" when dropping off my children? How is my day impacted when I start it with Scripture instead of social media? What are the Bible verses and stories that stick in your brain today? The repetition of hearing about Jonah and the whale or David and Goliath is truly meaningful. These are accounts you'll remember for a lifetime, and they will comfort you when you least expect it.

A friend of mine and her husband perform a little word dance every night before bed. "I love you," she says. "I love you more," he always replies. Of course, he doesn't actually love her more than she loves him, but it is a meaningful exchange, ritualizing and rooting them in the truth of their love for one another.

Meaningful repetition embeds things in our brains, creating pathways toward joy and hope when nothing else can. We can craft purposeful lives aimed at a larger purpose by filling them with important practices that align with who God made us to be and who He is clearly calling us to be today.

The practice of attending church, like the practices of prayer, worship, and Scripture reading, is a foundational building block in a thriving faith.

"The most powerful movement of feeling with a liturgy," wrote George Eliot, "is the prayer which seeks for nothing special, but is a yearning to escape from the limitations of our own weakness and an invocation of all Good to enter and abide with us."[3]

When we have no words, liturgy speaks for us. When we are lost, our rituals pull us back on track. When we feel blinded by chaos, the prayers of old can guide us home. Implementing these God-based habits into our lives means that even when things unfurl, we still have access to an internal, guiding force that always points us back to Him.

The rhythms of church life and community hold an extraordinary amount of abiding meaning and will be a lifeline—a thread that pulls you through even when you can't see it at the time. If you have young children now, you have

a beautiful opportunity to build foundational spiritual practices into their lives in addition to rebuilding them in your
own. Creating the patterns of faith may be one of the most
important things parents ever do for their children.

CHAPTER 23

Our World

CLINGING TO HOPE
DURING UNCERTAIN TIMES

As I write this, the country recently experienced a horrific event: Rioters overtook the Capitol building, forcing lawmakers and staffers to hide in fear for their lives. Given what could happen in a situation like that, no one knew what would ensue.

Videos have emerged of Congress members crouching on the floor while United States Representative Lisa Blunt Rochester proclaimed a prayer:

Father God, You are all powerful. We know that all things work together for the good. So we are trusting You right now in the name of Jesus—that You have this under control. We are trusting You right now, in the name of Jesus.[1]

God used this sister in Christ to comfort and calm those around her. In that same hour, I saw a tweet from an agnostic writer processing the riot. She said that as an atheist, because prayer was off the table, she felt entirely helpless. I can imagine the despair of feeling like you're at the mercy of the universe alone.

Tragedy and transition, trials and terror: These things always draw people back to the Church, tickling their hope that faith really matters after all. Following the 9/11 terrorist attacks, 90 percent of Americans said that they dealt with the aftermath with prayer, church, or religion.[2]

In 1999, when the Columbine school shooting took place, I was in high school and felt the effects of it viscerally. I poured over reports about teenager Rachel Scott, who was murdered for allegedly saying that she believed in God when asked. It was later revealed that she had written in her journal, "I am not going to apologize for speaking the name of Jesus. . . . If I have to sacrifice everything . . . I will."[3]

Learning about her life jump-started my faith back into action at the time. I wrote an article about it for my school paper and contemplated what really mattered—and the finiteness of life—for the first time. If it could happen to her, across the country at a public high school, it could happen to me, too. Tragedy and fear have a way of nudging us to cling to God.

A couple of decades later, the pandemic had us all reevaluating our lives. Whether or not you were personally affected by death in the last several years, you were forced to consider it more seriously. With this in mind, how can we incorporate faith back into our lives, leaving behind past narratives or excuses as we do so?

With so many things collapsing around us, we need to understand how and why the local church and our global Church brothers and sisters matter. As I write, Kabul, Afghanistan has just fallen, and Hurricane Ida has left over a million people without power in New Orleans. Can being part of a local church really do anything to relieve this kind of suffering? Why *would* the Church thrive amid all this harm?

Statistics tell us that Christianity is losing steam in the West but that many people in non-Western nations are turning to God in tragedy. As Kabul fell in 2021, Christian leaders in Afghanistan reported from one underground church network that their 320-person group had rapidly expanded to approximately 2,500 in just two weeks.[4] Meanwhile, Pew Research Center projects that the number of Christians in Sub-Saharan Africa will grow to nearly 1.9 billion by 2050.[5]

While the West flees from God, much of the world runs toward Him. It's in this action, and in the following Scripture, that I find comfort. In Matthew 16:18 (NLT), Jesus says, "Upon this rock I will build my church, and all the powers of hell will not conquer it."

When we see so many around us turning away from God, it can be easy to feel like we are the ones who have been misled. But take heart by looking to your fellow brothers and sisters across the world. Many of them are enduring the hardship of what it means to be a Christian and are only growing stronger in their faith. That is a testimony to be taken seriously.

We *can* stay rooted in the fruit of the Spirit, just as we see the global Church doing. In times of trial, we should remind ourselves that there is no natural disaster, terrorist attack, or cultural moment that can break the Church or God's sovereignty over the world at large.

I hope this encourages your desire to improve your relationship with God and to draw strength from those who find Him so valuable that they put even their lives in jeopardy for Him.

After the atomic bombs were dropped near the end of World War II, C. S. Lewis wrote, "Do not let us begin by exaggerating the novelty of our situation." The world has been here before—through plagues and annihilations, human tragedy and mortal dangers. And yet, as Lewis went on, "the first action to be taken is to pull ourselves together." He continued,

> If we are all going to be destroyed by an atomic
> bomb, let that bomb when it comes find us doing
> sensible and human things—praying, working,
> teaching, reading, listening to music, bathing the
> children, playing tennis, chatting to our friends over
> a pint and a game of darts—not huddled together
> like frightened sheep and thinking about bombs.
> They may break our bodies (a microbe can do that)
> but they need not dominate our minds.[6]

Rather than let our spirits be mauled by the inevitable pain of the world, may we let our lives expand with the knowledge of a God who is bigger than all of it. Let us remember that this short time on earth is but a whisper compared to eternity spent experiencing the glory and goodness of a place where body and soul cannot be destroyed. (See Matthew 10:28.)

We can see this lived out in nations where people are hungry for the Lord in their hardship. Many such Christians face persecution for practicing their faith. *Christianity Today* found that "40 percent of the world faces significant hindrance in worshiping God freely."[7] And in 2020, the number of Christians killed for their faith rose by 60 percent.[8]

We are blessed to be able to freely commune with other believers and to have many options when it comes to when and where to do so. We can recognize the privilege we have in America to worship and gather in the light of day while dozens of Chinese Christians share one Bible, trading it back and forth for consumption and meeting under the cover of night. A Christian in those circumstances could quietly live out a personal relationship with God alone lest neighbors or government officials discover their faith. But they don't. For some reason, they are compelled to live the Christian life in community by sharing the gospel and "not neglecting to meet together" (Hebrews 10:25, ESV). Our brothers and sisters in Christ across the globe find it worth facing punishment and persecution to do this. It's important to ask why. Why would they risk their lives this way while some American Christians don't think we even need church to have a relationship with God?

Why aren't we doing what they're doing when we have

every opportunity to do so safely? The Church, despite its many failures, is a gift that offers us an opportunity to participate powerfully in the grand story God is writing.

Are we Christians in name only? *Cultural Christianity* is a term that describes the lifestyle of those who uphold many typical Christian values and identify as Christians but don't live out authentic relationships with Christ. In today's America, such a concept is waning. It's great to have Christian values permeate society, and as today's culture is losing its former attachment to these values, parts of society are sliding into decline. Just as many local churches are doing, we as individual Christians can adjust our faith practices. We can be part of positive change in this cultural moment rather than being swept away by the tide.

There's nothing Satan would like more than for people to believe that churches are dying and there's no hope of finding one that will have you. Don't fall for it. It's true that some church denominations are dying, but remember that newer churches—as diverse and varied as you can imagine—are opening to replace them. This is a great thing for people seeking a fresh faith community. God has never been constrained by headlines or statistics, and He defies them even in the face of our rapidly changing culture. The gates of the Church remain wide open, and the invitation to be part of it is always there.

Meanwhile, if you are still feeling locked in or attached to a church from your past, please know that that particular body does not have to be your destiny.

CHAPTER 24

Our Futures

OUR CHURCH PAST
ISN'T OUR CHURCH FUTURE

Most of us have stories about the churches we grew up in that make us wince when we think about them today. Maybe those are what caused you to leave or what make you hesitant about returning.

Remember: The church of your past isn't the church of your future. Write this truth down. Believe it. Make decisions based on it. Get rid of the distorted blueprint you see as the Church. If you had a bad experience with it, do everything you can to ensure that the next generation doesn't.

Put Not Your Faith in Men or Structures

Our faith is best shaped when we put Jesus first. When our eyes are on Him, and on bettering our relationship with

Him, we will naturally drop the man-made structures of our past faith that are no longer serving us or Him. The better you know Jesus, the freer you become from your past.

Faith built on the words of people or the worship of particular churches will ultimately fail us. We see this again and again. When we learn of the transgressions of trusted Christian leaders, it can be a struggle to comprehend that those once seen by many as faithful followers of Jesus have committed grave sins. But experiencing this has confirmed something for me: We can never put our faith in people. They'll always fail us somewhere along the way—even the ones we hold in the highest regard.

This is why we need to seek God ourselves, not merely rely on others to dictate our faith. Our church communities can help us, but we must personally pursue God's voice. He is a personal God who will lead us, but we have to be listening in order to hear Him. God's voice doesn't usually take the form of a flashy message in the sky. It often sounds like a simple urging in our hearts—a whisper requiring our stillness. The whisper may tell us to move on or try again or start something new.

A pastor once told me, "Churches aren't meant to last. They are here to do what they are here to do for a time and then move on." New churches are new earth, welcoming new life by necessity. Are you ready for fresh ground?

A Past I Pushed Against

You have the power to change the trajectory of a past narrative. I've done it with food and church and shame. Every story can change, as long as we are still breathing life into it.

The fifteen years I spent suffering from an eating disorder grew out of distorted thinking pushed on me by a toxic, body-obsessed culture. I'd been taught that my body must be slim and tight, that my beauty as a woman depended on how flat my stomach was. I learned that French fries were bad and carrot sticks were good, that deprivation was a fruit of the Spirit and indulgence was a deadly sin.

Then a religious program for dieting plunged me into deeper guilt for "not allowing" God to free me from my addiction. This spiritually wayward guidance from Christians I trusted only made things worse for my mental state.

Eventually I made my way to a therapist who began to help me reorder my mindset around food. When she asked me what I ate on a typical day, I recognized a problem immediately: I never ate breakfast, rarely had lunch, and lived off sugar-free lattes and Orbit gum. It made sense that I was starving every afternoon, barely able to control binge episodes.

The unexamined can be a hindrance. It can take us miles down the wrong road without our even realizing it. I didn't recognize what I was doing to myself until I laid out the actions that had been leading to bingeing. Examination is the blueprint to healing.

I didn't know then that there was a different story yet to develop—one I could and would write myself with God's help. Like my issues with food and my body, I had to give my faith story the time and curiosity it deserved to be processed and preserved.

In regard to my eating disorder, I came out well on the other side. Slowly, with the aid of therapy, books, support groups, and time, my perspective shifted. The embedded, disordered thinking took some major overhauling to set straight. I had to take a step back and reevaluate my mutated beliefs. But I kept trekking toward freedom, believing that the God I had loved since childhood could help me change the narratives.

Whatever past narratives you struggle with, you can follow the same process. If you desire to recapture your faith but feel unable to move forward, I'm here to say that it's possible.

Perhaps it's reviving that childlike faith you once had that will push you forward. "The Kingdom of God belongs to those who are like these children," says Jesus in Mark 10:14-15 (NLT). "I tell you the truth, anyone who doesn't receive the Kingdom of God like a child will never enter it."

As kids, we believe our parents when they tell us we'll be protected and loved. As children of God, we can believe Him when He says there is freedom in Christ. This verse reminds me that it's okay to fully put our trust in Him. The world will tell us that the answer lies within ourselves, that we are "enough" if only we believe that we are. But as Christians we know that only God is enough to save us from ourselves. As Sharon Hodde Miller writes, "'You are enough' in the same way that a loaf of bread and a fish was enough."[1]

In other words, our little offerings will multiply exponentially only when we offer them up to the Father. And bit by bit, in our offerings, in seeking and accepting grace and in giving ourselves margin, we will begin to see growth.

With permission to seek and ask and explore, we can find

freedom. With food, I realized that it was okay to eat what I wanted. With church, it was okay to not fully understand the doctrine of hell. Food wasn't my enemy—and neither was my pastor.

There is so much we can do to begin to truly know the heart of God for ourselves. Because others taught me things that were not fully aligned with the truth about Him, it felt off—because it *was* off. And it was only when I charted my own course through wrongheaded biblical teachings that I began to see that God wasn't who I'd always been told He was. That's why it's so important for us to keep our eyes on Him and His leading first, before any human teacher.

When I began to be intentional about how I conducted my faith life, it became more satisfying and nourishing. I was able to plan, make better choices, and anticipate their positive outcomes. Spiritual scaffolding began to hold me together, and my goal to grow in Christ became more apparent.

Have you evaluated your intentions? Taken an exploratory look at the faith of your past? Have you opened yourself up to the idea that maybe what you once knew is only one way of practicing faith?

CHAPTER 25

Our Calling

WHY THE CHURCH NEEDS US

There are no insignificant members of the family of God. Each one of us has a role to play, and there are a few key reasons your presence as a woman in God's family matters greatly in the local church.

1. **The local church is incomplete without you.** As a Christian, you are chosen by God, and that is a huge privilege. Your calling is not an accident but an intentional choice made by God. He created you specifically with a part to play in mind, a part that would build and edify His Church. As Sam Allberry writes, "You are not

less integral to the body of the church than anyone else. God does not make redundant Christians."[1]

Women have many gifts that bring deep value to the Church, including leading, speaking, offering wisdom, prophesying, and exercising hospitality. We can't care as well for each other as church members if everyone isn't playing their God-given role.

2. **Your personal growth matters beyond you.** Because you are an integral part of the body of Christ, your spiritual growth matters to others. When you aren't growing in your identity as a Christian, the overall growth of the Church is stunted as well. It's not that God isn't sovereign, but when His people aren't thriving, neither is His body. Throughout Scripture, we see God empowering women to fulfill His purposes. His confidence and trust in them show us that He believed that each one could specifically make a difference for the Kingdom.

3. **Your encouragement is important.** When you don't show up at church, you're deprived of godly encouragement from others, and those people miss out on the blessing of encouragement from you. Your personal experiences and voice as a woman are no accident. God places people in each of our paths for us to minister to specifically, often turning our tough past situations into opportunities to care for and speak into people when they most need it. Being available to be used by God in this way is an honor.

4. **The local church needs your help to make disciples.**
   One of the last things Jesus said before ascending into
   heaven after His resurrection was to "go and make
   disciples of all nations" (Matthew 28:19). That's a
   command for all of us. But obeying it is not a straight-
   forward process. Disciples—Jesus followers—are
   made organically through relationships, mentorships,
   and lasting commitments to pray. One of the most
   important (but often neglected) aspects of church culture is discipleship. The Church needs more women
   to step up and disciple those in the next generation.

5. **You are the only one with your perspective.** Our life
   experiences shape our views of church and faith. The
   premise of the local church remains the same, but
   there is always room for improvement or additional
   insight. A single mom I once met told me that years
   earlier she'd discovered that her church had no out-
   reach program to minister to single moms. This led
   her to create Single Mom Ministries, which is now a
   thriving organization partnering with churches across
   the nation! You can help reveal a gap in ministry just
   by being there. Rather than letting the local church go
   astray on certain issues, your perspective can shape it
   to go in a better direction.

Jesus said, "Follow me" (Matthew 4:19). His early disciples had no idea what this would mean, but they dropped

everything and walked with Him in faith. He is still asking people to follow Him today. Our voices, ideas, and presence matter in the community of believers, which is sorely lacking without us.

The local church needs you. Your specific call may not be as grand as starting your *own* church (though keep an open mind!), but it could be to help change the one in your community for the better. Instead of walking away from this place—even though that might be easier!—aim to participate in it in a way that honors God and shapes it for the better.

The spark of life you're feeling in your faith right now is an opportunity to make a difference for you and for the coming generations—those who will lead the Church of the future.

You are here, striving to know more intimately the One who has chosen you. You can be confident that this desire isn't a figment of your imagination because Jesus tells us, "You did not choose me, but *I chose you*" (John 15:16, emphasis added).

The reason you are drawn to God is because He chose you. And guess what? You chose Him back the moment you became a Christian. He's drawing you to Him, and as tough as past circumstances and current fellow Christians can sometimes be, He's letting you know that the Church is where He dwells. He never takes back the claim that the Church is His body on earth today. As part of God's body here on earth, your presence is indispensable.

You've been chosen to participate in this experiment of

love on earth. In 1 Thessalonians 1:4, Paul says, "We know, brothers and sisters loved by God, that he has chosen you." You are loved by God, and He has chosen you to carry out His plans within His Church and beyond it.

"There are many who believe this and want change [in the Church]," writes Francis Chan. "The good news is that God wants this change even more than we do. And He doesn't just want these changes, He commands them! We can move forward in confidence, knowing God wouldn't command us to do something unless He also empowered us for the task."[2]

Reading this was a relief for me. I felt called to write this book, to help uplift the Church in society and among the women I know and love. The only reason I've been able to do that is because God has empowered me for the task. God will not ask you to do something without empowering you through His Spirit. The claim that "God will not give you something you can't handle" is false, but He will not give you something *He* can't or won't handle.

Such a realization energizes me to continue participating in the transformation of the local church into an entity even closer to what God intends it to be. As Christians, we can't run away from the Church. It's part of who we are, an essential component of our spiritual DNA. It's embedded in our souls. That's why you feel like you're missing a limb when you aren't a part of it (and why it's missing a limb when you aren't there!). God might be calling you to use *your* voice to enhance the future of the Christian faith and the local church for the next generation.

Following God Where He Leads

Jennie Allen is a bestselling Christian author and the founder of the popular IF:Gathering women's conference. But before the books, the conference, the speaking, the podcasts, and the Bible studies, Jennie went on a wild adventure with God. She boldly declared the word *anything* to Him, saying that she would follow His lead into *anything*. Ultimately this became the title of an incredible book, but when she said it that first time, it was scary.

At first, nothing happened, and Jennie wondered if she'd been mistaken about just what might be in store. But soon she heard God whisper, *Disciple a generation.* She had no idea what that meant for her exactly—or how to tackle the call—but ultimately the IF:Gathering formed in her mind, and step by step, in graceful humility, she built one of the most popular women's conferences in the country. She doesn't like to be in the spotlight—she'd rather sit back and watch other incredible women shine on stage—but her call to this ministry has changed lives and shown her what happens when we hear the voice of God and simply follow Him.[3]

Another Christian woman I once met also heeded this call to "anything." When she prayed for God to guide her, she ended up inside a prison. Various prison ministries have been around for years, but when this woman did some research, she found that none of them were focused specifically on the discipleship aspect of being the Church, which is key to our growth as Christians. She knew there were prisoners serving time who already knew Jesus—and she felt that they were the key to equipping and making a difference for the Church inside the prison walls. She created a ministry called Mercy Unleashed that seeks out Christian prisoners who can help disciple new Christians on the inside, holding church services and small groups on a regular basis.

"God's purpose in *all this* was to use the church to display his wisdom in its rich variety to all the unseen rulers and authorities in the heavenly places," says Paul in Ephesians 3:10 (NLT, emphasis added). "All this" reminds me of our lives; the mess of ourselves is where God's purpose is meant to be. He wants to use us to display His wisdom "in its rich variety." And He plans to do this through a rich variety of women like you and me.

What if these women hadn't listened to or obeyed God? Certainly God moves whether we move or not, but what an honor to be a part of His plan, which is much larger than us.

CHAPTER 26

Our Dreams

MAPPING OUT A PLAN

As you know by now, many women often don't prioritize the things we find most important or are most intuitively drawn toward, like faith. Even women who list "career" *last* on a list of things to improve spend the bulk of their time focusing on it. Meanwhile, most women who say they want to give more time to their faith lives allocate little attention there.[1]

The actions necessary to jump-start your spiritual life again take energy. Will you keep avoiding them? If so, at what cost? Do you want to live the rest of your life being pushed around by emotions and circumstances? Maybe it's time to chart a path toward something more fulfilling and meaningful instead.

If tragedy or the pandemic or setback or hardship teach us anything, it's that life is short and much of our busyness has little value long-term.

There's been a fanaticism about minimalism over the past few years. This isn't just about tangible clutter. It reveals that we need to reorganize our brains and structure our lives around the core components that make us human: God, community, compassion, love.

We each need a distinct vision for what we want so we can work to make it a reality. Have you visualized the faith you want? Mapped it out, created a dream board, cultivated steps to move toward it? What would your life look like if you put what you know to be good into practice? Part of this is simply habit creation. Implementing faith-related action habits (like daily Bible reading, weekly church attendance, and regular prayer time) will bring about meaningful results. Envision what you want your relationship with God to look like and then watch as the power of intentional, consistent investment in your faith takes root over time.

You can keep barreling through life at a hundred miles an hour or you can create your own journey. Stop and take time to reconfigure your priorities and craft a better, more fulfilling and satisfying life with holistic faith at the core. It's critical that you put Jesus at the center first and foremost and then work outward from there.

Visualizing this on paper could be key to bringing it to fruition. Tangible objects and visualizations help make ideas and concepts stick more firmly in our minds.[2]

Consider the symbolism found in Christianity: fish, loaves, coins, sheep, wine. It's because we can wrap our minds around these objects that we remember the lessons that accompany them. The same can be true when it comes to mapping out the faith life you hope to live. When you associate an image—a tangible symbol of the future you are striving for—with a goal, the goal becomes that much more real.

Grab materials for a dream board or start a bullet journal listing specific steps to take toward your goal. Here are a few ideas to get you started:

1. List a few goals you have for the shift you'd like to make.

2. Find images and photos that visualize the traits and qualities that represent what you want (e.g., consistency, community, joy, contentment).

3. Identify two to three key Bible verses to be your focus, and write them on the board or in the journal.

4. Add quotes that encourage or motivate you.

5. Identify "mentors from afar"—faith leaders you'd like to emulate.

6. Brainstorm small habits you can form to help you move forward.

Just like with any other kind of goal, goals for our spiritual lives can have structure, milestones, and moments of achievement. Some people don't like to think about spiritual goals this way: "Shouldn't they just be natural?" For some believers maybe. But I heard the same thing about dating when I was in my twenties—people didn't want to try online dating because it "wasn't natural." But I met my husband on Match.com, and neither of us cares that it wasn't "natural." It's a pathway toward a goal. In that case, marriage. In this case, a deeper relationship with God.

Most people aren't doing this. But you aren't most people. Don't stay stuck; this is your opportunity to pivot. Deep dive into the life of the One you follow, and take notes. As I've said, you can have a relationship with Jesus and be a Christian outside of church attendance—that much is clear. But the local church is often the cornerstone of everything else in our spiritual lives. Christians who don't attend church are less likely to read the Bible, pray, volunteer, or give charitably— and all those things matter.

Leaving church, or even attending without intention, slowly forms us into people we'd rather not be. Our faith practices root us in meaningful rhythms that shape our lives for the better, and the local church is one of the most powerful.

If you have accepted Jesus as your Savior, you are chosen. There is no greater honor and privilege. That is a calling in and of itself—a pathway to peace and purpose here on earth. So what do you do with it? I recommend that you start listening for God's voice with an open heart by reading Scripture, studying Jesus' life, and engaging with trusted

Christian friends. You can start with an online community, but take those conversations offline as soon as you can.

How Is God Speaking to You?

If you aren't sure what you're hearing from God right now, there are a few ways to look for clarity. I love asking people how they hear from God personally—and the answer is usually some iteration of *in a still, small voice*. There aren't usually any literal burning bushes these days, but there are figurative ones. God wants to talk to you. He *is* talking to you, through this book, through His Word, and in your daily life. Here are a few ways to find out whether you are hearing Him accurately:

- **Scripture.** You've heard it before, but that's because it's true. I recently read through the whole Bible in one year—an incredible experience that showed me aspects of God's character I hadn't known about despite spending my entire life as a Christian. A verse you've read a hundred times can spark to life with new meaning when God has something to say to you. Regular Scripture reading gives you the opportunity to hear from God every single day. Isaiah says that God's Word "will not return to [God] empty, but will . . . achieve the purpose for which [He] sent it" (Isaiah 55:11). This is huge—don't neglect it.

- **Prayer.** I highly recommend praying out loud or in writing. Sometimes when I'm praying out loud the conversation goes in a direction that totally catches me off guard. Suddenly, I'm reciting words and promises of God back to myself, specific things that comfort that guide me just the way I need. I've found myself in tears more than once as I've realized that God is using my own prayers to speak to me about particular situations.

• **Worship music.** There is a time to turn on the Pandora worship station and let it roll. I've heard it said that worry and worship can't happen at the same time. Try it, and you'll see what I mean. Worship music has a supernatural presence that blocks out the negativity of the world.

• **Teaching our kids.** Since having kids, I've found myself explaining simple biblical stories and concepts anew. As I discover ways to strip my beliefs down to their essential elements—bite-sized bits for toddlers—I've come to recognize the foundational truths of what I believe more powerfully than ever.

For example, I've always struggled with the concept of eternity. But because my son has lots of questions about heaven (Can I live with you? Will Grandma be there? Will I be able to eat as many marshmallows as I want?), I've begun to find more peace about it than ever just by processing them. God speaks to me through the lessons I'm teaching my children because I must look to Him for the right words.

• **Other people.** Whether it's friends, family members, or pastors, God uses other people in our lives to speak to us every day. He can give people messages just for us, and He does so all the time through billboards, radio chats, podcasts, and even strangers. He will get His messages across; we just need to be open to them.

I heard one great example of this on a podcast episode featuring a woman named Brittany Price Brooker, who shared her story of losing her husband unexpectedly when their children were very small. In the days after his death, she was drowning in grief and in the difficulties of motherhood, crying out to God to show her He was there. On one particularly hard day—which happened to be Mother's Day—she was struggling to give her kids a bath when she broke down, saying, *God, will You show up? Do You really care about me as a mother?*

Seconds later, her doorbell rang. A friend who had five children of her own and lived forty-five minutes away was at the door. She said, "I know this is crazy, but about an hour ago, God told me to come to your house and help bathe your babies."

Brittany was in awe of the provision God had for her, directing a friend to her house an hour before her moment of need so she would arrive just as Brittany called out to Him.[3]

- **Nature.** Elements of God's creation touch people in specific ways. For me, it's hard to watch a pink-melon sunset without being in awe of God's glory. The glow of the sinking rays diminish my worries, at least for a moment. Sometimes we get so enveloped in our daily lives that we forget to take time to appreciate such scenes and recognize that God loves to speak to our hearts through them.

- **Silence.** Podcasts, TV shows, whiny kids, Spotify, Zoom meetings, you name it. Silence is a commodity these days. You have to intentionally cultivate it, and that's not always easy. But silencing our world makes space for God to speak. Sometimes when we don't feel like praying or know what to say, silence is the fastest track to clarity. Get quiet and let God help you hear what you need to hear in the moment.

This is certainly not an exhaustive list, but it might help. Sometimes it's overwhelming to think that we're supposed to just "hear God" somehow. By understanding that there are opportunities to do so every day and cultivating space for it in our lives, we will be more attuned to what He is saying.

Stop trying to do faith all on your own. You are not alone and were never intended to be. It's time to access the resources you have to find a church home you can live and thrive in.

CHAPTER 27

Our Destiny

MADE FOR THIS

Many women often say yes to too many things. By default, we can try to wear too many hats and end up burning out in the most important areas of life, including the places where our essential nourishment should be coming from. Is it a Western thing, a mom thing, an extrovert thing? I don't know, but whatever it is, it keeps us from living our best lives.

It's time. Are you ready to take what you've learned here and pare down your commitments so you can prioritize what matters? First, tally your priorities and values. Next, make a list of what actually gets done. Now compare these two lists. Is faith on the first list but not the second? If so, evaluate why, eliminate what you need to, and choose to change this reality.

It's time to rewrite our faith stories. We are not beholden to the past, and everyone who is in Christ is a "new creation" (2 Corinthians 5:17, ESV). The church of your past doesn't have to be the church of your future. Your past can't dictate anything without your permission; don't let it. Write yourself reminders that this is a new day in your life and things have shifted. Know this truth, believe it, and live it out.

I want to reclaim the Church for what it is: God's holy home on earth. We can overcome the past and create a different future, one dedicated to interpreting Scripture with discernment and filtering our faith through the lens of truth. The Church isn't defined by what people in your past have done but rather by what Jesus has done for you.

God has graciously allowed me to see misleading teaching as extreme human failure. Pastors and leaders are mere men and women. They *will* disappoint you. But we can trust the Bible's statement that "the foolishness of God is wiser than men, and the weakness of God is stronger than men" (1 Corinthians 1:25, NKJV). In other words, people are no substitute for and no representation of our ever-loving, wise, and all-powerful God.

If you need to wipe the slate clean when it comes to church, the time is now.

As moms and mentors, aunts and colleagues, sisters and friends, we want to teach the next generation about the reality of the human capacity for failure and the supreme truth that God is our only Redeemer.

Whether apathy, the pandemic, or past hurt is what has

taken you away from church, it's time to reclaim this part of your life. Reigniting your faith will move you closer to the best life God has for you.

There are likely several church communities within driving distance of your home. In these pages, you've met people who have started off as members of one denomination and ended up in another. You've read about folks with painful church pasts who are able to see beyond the hurt and into the church family that God intends for them.

As the local church continues to adapt to the changing culture, there will be more and more room for those on the margins and in other hard places to step in and address the deep spiritual longing we are all born with.

"My soul yearns for you in the night; in the morning my spirit longs for you," says Isaiah 26:9. God created us for deep, lasting relationships with Him and others. He put within us a yearning that cannot be fulfilled by any other means but the community of believers. It's part of how we know Him intimately.

When Jesus walked on the earth, He never became a lead pastor. He never marked out a building as His church or approved a specific kind of pulpit. I imagine He would have cringed at standing behind one. He had no interest in fame.

Jesus wanted to know the people around Him, and He did so just by being present—sitting in a circle beneath towering cedar trees or side by side with sinners on a rocking boat. Perhaps He huddled under a tiny shelter, raindrops pelting the ground as His friends leaned closer to hear the holiest words ever uttered. To have the great fortune of being on earth with Jesus? What an honor. But honestly, not much has changed.

God still meets us in storms and on the tops of mountains, in the middle of our blindness and our disease and our grief and our sin. He still meets us when we are together, a striving bunch of Jesus followers just trying to live and love as He calls us.

When Jesus left earth at age thirty-three, He didn't leave us a conference or a podcast or a Bible study series. He didn't start a network or an email list or a clothing line. He left a community. The members were rough and tumble. They screwed up, and they're still screwing up. Jesus knew they would but loved them anyway. He saved them anyway. He wanted to be with them anyway. He still wants to be with them anyway.

The Church is so much more than just a structure. What is it? It's a group of people sitting around a kitchen table being willing to offer up their brokenness before one another and admit they don't have anything figured out. It's these people showing up when they've got nothing to say but need someone else to hold them up. It's about believing God when He says we need one another.

It's a holy community of imperfect saints traveling together toward the Holy City.

Won't you join us?

Notes

INTRODUCTION

1. Another name for the hymn "Why Should I Feel Discouraged" by Civilla D. Martin.

CHAPTER 1 | OUR DESIRES: SEARCHING FOR MORE

1. For percentages of US women attending church weekly in 2010 and 2020 respectively, see Ryan Burge, "Guest Column: Behind the Steep Decline in Church Attendance Among Women," Barna, March 4, 2020, https://www.barna.com/changes-behind-the-scenes. For the population of women in the US during those same years, see "Total Population in the United States by Gender from 2010 to 2025," Statista, accessed February 11, 2022, https://www.statista.com/statistics/737923/us-population-by-gender.

2. See, for example, Nicole F. Roberts, "Science Says: Religion Is Good for Your Health," *Forbes*, March 29, 2019, https://www.forbes.com/sites/nicolefisher/2019/03/29/science-says-religion-is-good-for-your-health; and Shanshan Li et al., "Religious Service Attendance and Lower Depression among Women—a Prospective Cohort Study," *Annals of Behavioral Medicine* 50, no. 6 (December 2016): 876–84, https://www.ncbi.nlm.nih.gov/pmc/articles/PMC5127763.

3. Mark Sayers, *Reappearing Church: The Hope for Renewal in the Rise of Our Post-Christian Culture* (Chicago: Moody, 2019), 118.

4. Barna Group, *Churchless: Understanding Today's Unchurched and How*

to Connect with Them, ed. George Barna and David Kinnaman (Carol Stream, IL: Tyndale Momentum, 2014), 48.

5. Barna, *Churchless*, 52.

6. Blue Letter Bible, "Lexicon: Strong's G1577—*ekklēsia*," accessed February 11, 2022, https://www.blueletterbible.org/lexicon/g1577/niv/mgnt/0-1.

7. Sam Allberry, *Why Bother with Church? And Other Questions about Why You Need It and It Needs You* (Epsom, Surrey, UK: The Good Book Company, 2006), 17.

8. Allberry, *Why Bother*, 129.

9. C. S. Lewis, *The Problem of Pain* (New York: HarperOne, 2013), 155.

CHAPTER 2 | OUR TIME: DO WE HAVE ENOUGH FOR GOD?

1. Josie Cox, "Why Women Are More Burned Out Than Men," BBC, October 3, 2021, https://www.bbc.com/worklife/article/20210928-why -women-are-more-burned-out-than-men.

2. "Five Factors Changing Women's Relationship with Churches," Barna, June 25, 2015, https://www.barna.com/research/five-factors-changing -womens-relationship-with-churches.

3. According to a series of Barna studies conducted between 1993 and 2015, 22 percent of the women surveyed who wanted to improve in at least one life area identified "church or religious activities" as that area for improvement. See Barna, "Five Factors."

4. Rachel Mayew, "Clearing Self-Limiting Beliefs," Holistic Faith Lifestyle, accessed February 11, 2022, https://holisticfaithlifestyle.com/self-limiting -beliefs.

5. Jen Wilkin, *Women of the Word: How to Study the Bible with Both Our Hearts and Our Minds* (Wheaton, IL: Crossway, 2014), 78.

6. Tony Evans (@drtonyevans), Twitter, July 31, 2021, 10:47 a.m., https://twitter.com/drtonyevans/status/1421512764703580161.

CHAPTER 3 | OUR MISCONCEPTIONS: WE DON'T NEED CHURCH TO HAVE A RELATIONSHIP WITH GOD

1. Barna, "Five Factors Changing Women's Relationship with Churches," June 25, 2015, https://www.barna.com/research/five-factors-changing -womens-relationship-with-churches.

CHAPTER 4 | OUR UNDERSTANDING: WHAT IS THE CHURCH TO US?

1. For "See You at the Pole"; see syatp.com.

2. Aaron Earls, "22 Vital Stats for Ministry in 2022," Lifeway Research, January 5, 2022, https://research.lifeway.com/2022/01/05/22-vital-stats -for-ministry-in-2022.

3. Ed Stetzer, "Survey Fail—Christianity Isn't Dying," *USA Today*, May 13, 2015, https://www.usatoday.com/story/opinion/2015/05/13/nones -americans-christians-evangelicals-column/27198423.

4. See https://freshexpressionsus.org/about/#why.

5. See https://www.facebook.com/speedwayracingministries.

6. Emily Jensen and Laura Wifler, *Risen Motherhood: Gospel Hope for Everyday Moments* (Eugene, OR: Harvest House, 2019), 149.

7. "Seeing the Forest for All the Trees: Tree Species Do Better Together," Scimex, February 28, 2017, https://www.scimex.org/newsfeed/seeing -the-forest-for-all-the-trees-tree-species-do-better-together.

CHAPTER 5 | OUR EXCUSES: A MILLION GOOD REASONS

1. Christine Tamir, Aidan Connaughton, and Ariana Monique Salazar, "The Global God Divide," Pew Research Center, July 20, 2020, https://www.pewresearch.org/global/2020/07/20/the-global-god-divide.

CHAPTER 6 | OUR PAIN: WHEN CHURCH HURT STILL HURTS

1. Jules Woodson, "I Was Assaulted. He Was Applauded," *New York Times*, March 9, 2018, https://www.nytimes.com/2018/03/09/opinion/jules -woodson-andy-savage-assault.html.

2. "Rachael Denhollander Speaks: Justice Matters," *Worth Your Time*, August 20, 2019, https://podcasts.apple.com/us/podcast/rachael -denhollander-speaks-justice-matters/id1443576278?i=1000447313926.

CHAPTER 7 | OUR PSYCHOLOGY: REPERCUSSIONS

1. Kendra Cherry, "The Role of a Schema in Psychology," Verywell Mind, updated September 23, 2019, https://www.verywellmind.com/what-is-a -schema-2795873.

2. *APA Dictionary of Psychology*, "schema," accessed January 25, 2022, https://dictionary.apa.org/schema.

3. Barna Group, *Churchless: Understanding Today's Unchurched and How to Connect with Them*, ed. George Barna and David Kinnaman (Carol Stream, IL: Tyndale Momentum, 2014), 4.

4. C. S. Lewis, *Letters to Malcolm, Chiefly on Prayer* (San Francisco: HarperOne, 2017), 2.

CHAPTER 8 | OUR MESSY LIVES: FINDING GRACE WHEN WE NEED IT MOST

1. "Why 2 Out of 3 Single Moms Don't Attend Your Church," The Life of a Single Mom, accessed January 19, 2022, https://thelifeofasinglemom.com /why-2-out-of-3-single-moms-don't-attend-your-church-by-jennifer-maggio.

2. C. H. Spurgeon, "Young Preachers Encouraged: A Short Address, Delivered to the Metropolitan Tabernacle Country Mission," *The Sword and the Trowel: A Record of Combat with Sin and Labour for the Lord*, ed. Charles Haddon Spurgeon (London: Passmore & Alabaster, 1881), 6.

CHAPTER 9 | OUR COMPLACENCY: WHEN WE FEEL SPIRITUALLY NUMB

1. "The Everlasting Man," *The Collected Works of G. K. Chesterton*, vol. 2 (San Francisco: Ignatius Press, 1986), 388.
2. C. S. Lewis, *Mere Christianity* (New York: HarperOne, 2017), 199.
3. Jen Wilkin, *Women of the Word: How to Study the Bible with Both Our Hearts and Our Minds* (Wheaton, IL: Crossway, 2014), 30.

CHAPTER 10 | OUR POLITICS: IS THIS A PROBLEM?

1. Katie Loveland, as quoted in Sarah Stankorb, "These Evangelical Women Are Abandoning Trump and Their Churches," *GEN*, July 22, 2020, https://gen.medium.com/these-evangelical-women-are-abandoning -trump-and-the-church-ee8899837fe.
2. As quoted in Kelsey Bolar, "The 'Shy Trump Voter' Is a Suburban Woman," *The Federalist*, November 12, 2020, https://thefederalist.com/2020/11/12 /the-shy-trump-voter-is-a-suburban-woman.
3. Not her real name.
4. Claire Gecewicz, "Many Churchgoers in U.S. Don't Know the Political Leanings of Their Clergy," Pew Research Center, January 13, 2020, https://www.pewresearch.org/fact-tank/2020/01/13/many-churchgoers -in-u-s-dont-know-the-political-leanings-of-their-clergy.
5. Megan Fowler, "Many Churchgoers Don't Know If Their Pastor Is a Republican or Democrat," *Christianity Today*, January 15, 2020, https://www.christianitytoday.com/news/2020/january/pew-churchgoers -dont-know-pastors-political-leanings.html.
6. According to a 2014 survey. See "Political Ideology among Christians," Pew Research Center, accessed January 19, 2022, https://www.pewforum .org/religious-landscape-study/christians/christian/political-ideology.
7. Mark Sayers, *Reappearing Church: The Hope for Renewal in the Rise of Our Post-Christian Culture* (Chicago: Moody, 2019), 48.
8. Lauren Chandler, *Steadfast Love* (Nashville: B&H, 2016), chap. 1.

CHAPTER 11 | OUR SPIRITUALITY: THE MISSING PIECE

1. Dallas Willard, *The Divine Conspiracy: Rediscovering Our Hidden Life in God* (San Francisco: HarperSanFrancisco, 1998), 77, emphasis added.
2. Willard, *Divine Conspiracy*, 83.

CHAPTER 12 | OUR QUESTIONS: THERE IS FREEDOM IN ASKING THEM

1. Rebecca McLaughlin, *Confronting Christianity: 12 Hard Questions for the World's Largest Religion* (Wheaton, IL: Crossway, 2019), 114.
2. William Bruce Cameron, *Informal Sociology: A Casual Introduction to Sociological Thinking* (New York: Random House, 1963), 13.
3. Marc Byrd and Steve Hindalong, "God of Wonders," *City on a Hill: Songs of Worship and Praise* © 2000 Essential Records.

CHAPTER 13 | OUR DISCOMFORT: HOW IT LEADS TO GROWTH

1. Hartford Institute for Religion Research, "Fast Facts about American Religion," accessed January 19, 2022, hirr.hartsem.edu/research/fastfacts/fast_facts.html.

CHAPTER 14 | OUR LONELINESS: COMBATING THE EPIDEMIC

1. A. H. Weinberger et al., "Trends in Depression Prevalence in the USA from 2005 to 2015: Widening Disparities in Vulnerable Groups," *Psychological Medicine* 48, no. 8 (2018): 1308–15, https://doi.org/10.1017/S0033291717002781.
2. "Depression in Women," Mental Health America, accessed January 20, 2022, https://www.mhanational.org/depression-women.
3. Jillian McKoy, "Depression Rates in US Tripled When the Pandemic First Hit—Now, They're Even Worse," The Brink, October 7, 2021, https://www.bu.edu/articles/2021/depression-rates-tripled-when-pandemic-first-hit.
4. Megan Brenan, "U.S. Mental Health Rating Remains Below Pre-Pandemic Level," Gallup, December 3, 2021, https://news.gallup.com/poll/357749/mental-health-rating-remains-below-pre-pandemic-level.aspx.
5. Johann Hari, *Lost Connections: Why You're Depressed and How to Find Hope* (London: Bloomsbury, 2020), 62, emphasis added.
6. Hari, *Lost Connections*, 52.
7. Timon Elmer and Christoph Stadtfeld, "Depressive Symptoms Are Associated with Social Isolation in Face-to-Face Interaction Networks," *Scientific Reports* 10, no. 1444 (2020), https://doi.org/10.1038/s41598-020-58297-9.
8. Johann Hari, "The Likely Cause of Addiction Has Been Discovered, and It Is Not What You Think," *HuffPost*, updated April 18, 2017, https://www.huffpost.com/entry/the-real-cause-of-addicti_b_6506936.
9. As noted in this article I wrote a few years ago: Ericka Andersen, "Is God the Answer to the Suicide Epidemic?" *Wall Street Journal*, July 11,

2019, https://www.wsj.com/articles/is-god-the-answer-to-the-suicide-epidemic-11562885290.

10. "Religion's Relationship to Happiness, Civic Engagement and Health Around the World," Pew Research Center, January 31, 2019, https://www.pewforum.org/2019/01/31/religions-relationship-to-happiness-civic-engagement-and-health-around-the-world.

CHAPTER 15 | OUR PEOPLE: WHAT HAPPENS WHEN WE GATHER

1. Brené Brown, *The Gifts of Imperfection*, 10th anniv. ed. (New York: Random House, 2020), 55.
2. Zach Hrynowski, "How Many Americans Believe in God?," Gallup, October 29, 2019, https://news.gallup.com/poll/268205/americans-believe-god.aspx.

CHAPTER 16 | OUR PRESENCE: SHOWING UP IS POWERFUL

1. Megan Hill, *A Place to Belong: Learning to Love the Local Church* (Wheaton, IL: Crossway, 2020), 26.
2. J. R. Briggs, *A Time to Heal: Offering Hope to a Wounded World in the Name of Jesus* (Oviedo, FL: HigherLife, 2021), 54.
3. Lore Ferguson Wilbert, *Handle with Care: How Jesus Redeems the Power of Touch in Life and Ministry* (Nashville: B&H, 2020), introduction.

CHAPTER 17 | OUR KIDS: WHY CHURCH MATTERS FOR THEM

1. According to a 2014 study. "Agnostics," Pew Research Center, accessed January 19, 2022, https://www.pewforum.org/religious-landscape-study/religious-family/agnostic.
2. "Children's Ministry Statistics (2019): How Do Kids Come to Christ?," Ministry-To-Children, updated February 5, 2022, https://ministry-to-children.com/childrens-ministry-statistics.
3. "Who Is Responsible for Children's Faith Formation?," Barna, March 19, 2019, https://www.barna.com/research/children-faith-formation.
4. Erica Komisar, "Don't Believe in God? Lie to Your Children," *Wall Street Journal*, December 5, 2019, https://www.wsj.com/articles/dont-believe-in-god-lie-to-your-children-11575591658.
5. Komisar, "Don't Believe in God?"
6. "What's with All the Deconstruction Stories?—With Sean McDowell," *The Alisa Childers Podcast*, September 20, 2020, https://www.alisachilders.com/blog/whats-with-all-the-deconstruction-stories-with-sean-mcdowell-the-alisa-childers-podcast-80.

7. *Alisa Childers Podcast*, "What's with All the Deconstruction Stories?"
8. Christine Caine (@ChristineCaine), Twitter, April 13, 2018, 12:10pm, https://twitter.com/ChristineCaine/status/984841161863987202.
9. "God Is Bigger Than the Boogie Man," *VeggieTunes* © 1995 Big Idea.

CHAPTER 18 | OUR BELONGING: A PLACE TO BE HELD

1. Stephen A. Smith (@stephenasmith), "We Don't Care," TikTok, October 15, 2020, https://www.tiktok.com/foryou?is_from_webapp =v1&item_id=6883957604855319813&lang=en#!/@stephenasmith /video/6883957604855319813.
2. Not her real name.
3. Lisa Cannon Green, "Survey: Women Go Silently from Church to Abortion Clinic," Focus on the Family, August 17, 2021, https://www.focusonthefamily.com/pro-life/survey-women-go -silently-from-church-to-abortion-clinic.
4. Megan Hill, *A Place to Belong: Learning to Love the Local Church* (Wheaton, IL: Crossway, 2020), chap. 2.

CHAPTER 20 | OUR COMMUNITY: FINDING THE RIGHT SPACE AND PLACE

1. C. S. Lewis, *Mere Christianity* (New York: HarperOne, 2017), chap. 1.
2. Mark Sayers, *Reappearing Church: The Hope for Renewal in the Rise of Our Post-Christian Culture* (Chicago: Moody, 2019), 117.
3. Alexandra Hoover, *Eyes Up: How to Trust God's Heart by Tracing His Hand* (Nashville: B&H, 2022).

CHAPTER 21 | OUR SOCIETY: HOW GOING TO CHURCH CHANGES THE WORLD

1. Jonathan Brooks, *Church Forsaken: Practicing Presence in Neglected Neighborhoods* (Downers Grove, IL: IVP Books, 2018), 70.
2. "New Report Finds Religious People Are More Likely to Donate," *Philanthropy Daily*, October 25, 2017, https://www.philanthropydaily .com/religious-philanthropy-faith.
3. Robert D. Putnam and David E. Campbell, *American Grace: How Religion Divides and Unites Us* (New York: Simon & Schuster, 2012), 448.
4. Putnam and Campbell, *American Grace*, 450.
5. Brett Pelham and Steve Crabtree, "Worldwide, Highly Religious More Likely to Help Others," Gallup, October 8, 2008, https://news.gallup .com/poll/111013/worldwide-highly-religious-more-likely-to-help -others.aspx.

6. Jim Jansen, "The Civic and Community Engagement of Religiously Active Americans," Pew Research Center, December 23, 2011, https://www.pewresearch.org/internet/2011/12/23/the-civic-and -community-engagement-of-religiously-active-americans.

7. Jedd Medefind, "Heritage Foundation Forum: How Faith, Foster Care, and Adoption Go Together," Christian Alliance for Orphans, June 23, 2018, https://cafo.org/2018/06/23/heritage-foundation-forum-how-faith -foster-care-and-adoption-go-together.

CHAPTER 22 | OUR RITUALS: BUILDING A MEANINGFUL LIFE

1. Casper ter Kuile, *The Power of Ritual: Turning Everyday Activities into Soulful Practices* (New York: HarperOne, 2021), 11.

2. Tish Harrison Warren, *Liturgy of the Ordinary: Sacred Practices in Everyday Life* (Downers Grove, IL: IVP Books, 2016), 117.

3. George Eliot, *Daniel Deronda* (New York: Penguin, 1995), 367.

CHAPTER 23 | OUR WORLD: CLINGING TO HOPE DURING UNCERTAIN TIMES

1. Watch the video here: https://faithfullymagazine.com/lisa-blunt-rochester -prayer.

2. Jeremy E. Uecker, "Religious and Spiritual Responses to 9/11: Evidence from the Add Health Study," *Sociological Spectrum* 28, no. 5 (2008): 477–509, https://www.ncbi.nlm.nih.gov/pmc/articles/PMC3118577.

3. Patricia Raybon, *The One Year God's Great Blessings Devotional: A Daily Guide* (Carol Stream, IL: Tyndale, 2011), October 11.

4. Eleventh Hour Worship (@eleventhhourworship), Instagram post, August 27, 2021, https://www.instagram.com/p/CTGHKAWH2HZ.

5. "The Future of World Religions: Population Growth Projections, 2010–2050," Pew Research Center, April 2, 2015, https://www.pewforum.org/2015/04/02 /christians.

6. C. S. Lewis, "On Living in an Atomic Age," *Present Concerns*, ed. Walter Hooper (San Diego: Harcourt Brace Jovanovich, 1987), 73–74.

7. Jayson Casper, "Pew and IDOP Agree: Religious Persecution Is Worsening Worldwide," *Christianity Today*, November 10, 2020, https://www.christianitytoday.com/news/2020/november/pew -christian-muslim-persecution-religion-report-idop.html.

8. Charlene Aaron, "Number of Christians Murdered for Faith Rose 60 Percent in 2020: List of Most Dangerous Places for Believers," *CBN News*, January 14, 2021, https://www1.cbn.com/cbnnews/cwn/2021 /january/1-in-8-christians-now-persecuted-for-their-faith-here-are-the -most-dangerous-countries-to-be-a-christian-in-2021.

CHAPTER 24 | OUR FUTURES: OUR CHURCH PAST ISN'T OUR CHURCH FUTURE

1. Sharon H. Miller (@sharonhmiller), Instagram post, December 4, 2021, https://www.instagram.com/p/CXEzGJ0J2fB.

CHAPTER 25 | OUR CALLING: WHY THE CHURCH NEEDS US

1. Sam Allberry, "Your Church Needs You This Sunday: Two Prayers to Prepare for Worship," Desiring God, January 5, 2020, https://www.desiringgod.org/articles/your-church-needs-you-this-sunday.
2. Francis Chan, *Letters to the Church* (Colorado Springs: David C Cook, 2018), 26–27.
3. Jennie shares about this in her book *Anything: The Prayer That Unlocked My God and My Soul* (Nashville: W Publishing Group, 2011).

CHAPTER 26 | OUR DREAMS: MAPPING OUT A PLAN

1. "Five Factors Changing Women's Relationship with Churches," Barna, June 25, 2015, https://www.barna.com/research/five-factors-changing-womens-relationship-with-churches.
2. Frank Niles, "How to Use Visualization to Achieve Your Goals," *HuffPost*, June 17, 2011, https://www.huffpost.com/entry/visualization-goals_b_878424.
3. "The Happy Hour #202 with Brittany Price Brooker," *The Happy Hour*, July 18, 2018, https://www.jamieivey.com/the-happy-hour-202-brittany-price-brooker.